59372083654353   POL

D0350060

ONLY THE CRAZY AND FEARLESS

WIN BIG!

THE SURPRISING SECRETS TO SUCCESS
IN BUSINESS AND IN LIFE

ARTHUR WYLIE

WITH BRIAN NICOL

BenBella

Copyright © 2011 by Arthur Wylie

All rights reserved. No part of this book may be used or reproduced in any manner whatsoever without written permission except in the case of brief quotations embodied in critical articles or reviews.

BENBELLA

BenBella Books, Inc.
10300 N. Central Expressway, Suite 400
Dallas, TX 75231
benbellabooks.com
Send feedback to feedback@benbellabooks.com

Printed in the United States of America

10 9 8 7 6 5 4 3 2 1

Library of Congress Cataloging-in-Publication Data
Wylie, Arthur.
Only the crazy and fearless win big! : the surprising secrets to success in business and in life / Arthur Wylie with Brian Nicol.
p. cm.
Includes bibliographical references and index.
ISBN 978-1-935618-49-2 (alk. paper)
1. Success in business. 2. Success. I. Nicol, Brian. II. Title.
HF5386.W957 2011
650.1—dc23
2011039148

Editing by Brian Nicol
Copyediting by Rebecca Logan
Cover design by Faceout Studio
Text design and composition by Neuwirth & Associates, Inc.
Printed by Bang Printing

Distributed by Perseus Distribution
perseusdistribution.com

To place orders through Perseus Distribution:
Tel: 800-343-4499
Fax: 800-351-5073
E-mail: orderentry@perseusbooks.com

Significant discounts for bulk sales are available. Please contact Glenn Yeffeth at glenn@benbellabooks.com or (214) 750-3628.

CONTENTS

INTRODUCTION

Detroit?! Michigan?! Industrial has-been. Urban wasteland. The Big Three on life support. Crime out of control. Unemployment through the roof. Neighborhoods abandoned. Politicians dishonest and corrupt. The city that lost 25 percent of its population from 2000 to 2010. *That* Detroit, Michigan?!

Yes, said my real estate advisor, that's the one. It was late 2009, in the throes of the Great Recession, and my advisor was recommending I build my movie studio complex in the Detroit area, in Allen Park on the city's edge. Before I could lodge my protests, he rattled off the benefits of the property: buildings and warehouses already there, including a jail and a courthouse perfect for filming, and a cafeteria and classrooms—a film school even. More than a hundred acres—it could be the biggest studio in the country.

But it's Detroit! Did he think I was crazy?!

Well, apparently I am. Because the next day I was at the site, being shown around by city officials, and within two weeks we were on the property. My Hollywood production company, Global Renaissance Entertainment Group, moved its headquarters to Allen Park and established the

Wylie Institute for the Study of Entrepreneurship and Wylie Studios. Six major films were soon slated to be made at the new facility within the coming three years. Arthur Wylie, the self-made business mogul from North Carolina, had put his money and reputation on the Detroit area. Detroit, the recession's ground zero, where four-bedroom houses were listed for $5,000 and still weren't selling, the place nobody wanted to move to and many wanted to abandon, if only they could.

A logical move? A smart decision? Maybe not at first blush. But my fearless and crazy instincts told me to go ahead, to strike the deal. In fact, a few of my business colleagues who admired the decision called me "fearless." Many more shook their heads and called me "crazy." But that decision (like this book) was based on the fact that sometimes the best decisions you'll ever make are fearless or crazy—or both.

Those hookers and pimps and garbage and guns I imagined everywhere on the streets of Detroit? Not so much. The city is recovering and reinventing itself. Major redevelopment projects are springing up. The downtown is revitalized and renewed. The auto industry is back with a vengeance. Detroit even promoted itself creatively during the 2011 Super Bowl and has continued since then with Chrysler's "Imported from Detroit" commercials.

It seemed like a good time to hang up my shingle in the Motor City.

And for this fearless and crazy entrepreneur, the story gets even better. The state of Michigan welcomed filmmakers with open arms and a fistful of dollars. It had some of the most generous film industry tax incentives in the country, with a refundable tax credit of up to 42 percent for production expenses. That means if I made a $10 million movie in Michigan, I would get back as much as $4.2 million after completing the film. Now *that's* an incentive. I got so excited that I told my team, "We're not going to Michigan just to make movies; we're going to make history!"

Arthur Wylie fearless and crazy? You bet—all the way to the bank.

I'm not unique, of course, and that's the message of this book. The first question I ask any mega-successful person I meet is, "What's the craziest or most fearless thing you ever did to make money?"

Do they think my question rude, intrusive? Not at all. In fact, they can't wait to tell me. And as you might expect, their answers vary widely. Yet the things these entrepreneurs have in common are striking. What I notice about these people is this:

- They never settle for being just good enough.
- They take advantage of opportunities they are passionate about.
- They always start with small goals and build to something big.
- They take chances even when the rule book tells them to play it safe.
- They listen to their gut, not to what others say is proper and prudent.

Some of the most successful people I know—most of them, in fact—are prouder of the fearless and crazy things they've done than they are of all their logical, orderly, rational decisions.

Setting up shop in the Detroit area wasn't my first fearless and crazy decision. Far from it. In fact, I got my start by making such decisions. I began what eventually became my $475 million financial services company, Arthur Wylie Wealth Management—an enterprise that managed assets and transactions throughout the United States—in my college dorm room in the 1990s. And I did it with a stack of fresh credit cards. As I'm sure you'll recall, credit card companies were marketing themselves everywhere and anywhere in those days, including on college campuses. You could pick up simple card applications at just about any restaurant, shop, or gas station. It was the old-school American way—not a good plan for building a satisfying, wealthy life. In fact, a warning: Kids, don't try this at home, or in your own career.

Anyway, I was sitting in a Chinese restaurant one day when I noticed my first credit card promotional flyer; it was for a MasterCard. I filled it out, placed it on the table between my wonton soup and kung pao chicken, and started doing the math. If I got a few hundred or a few thousand dollars in credit on every card I applied for, I could have access to tens of thousands of dollars in no time. By the time I bit into my almond cookie, I was hooked.

I soon noticed that every Chinese restaurant or locally owned food shop had a similar flyer offering a free application for a credit card. It seemed like each place had a different offer, and needless to say, I spent a lot of that summer eating Chinese food and filling out credit card applications.

Once the cards started rolling in, I had access to more than $100,000 in untapped credit. I charged some office supplies, installed a few phone lines, printed up some business cards, and—*boom*—Arthur Wylie Wealth Management was born right there in the dorms of the University of North Carolina– Charlotte (UNCC).

It worked; the company quickly blossomed. I was able to juggle my credit payments and finesse my debt—until I finally didn't need all that plastic anymore.

But in the wealth management business, you're only as successful as your clients, and in fact, you can have success only if you *have* clients. The treadmill was relentless. If I stood still, I was losing ground. I had always preached "residual" income when I gave financial advice—income that would keep on flowing after the creative work, the hard stuff, was done. Now I wanted some for myself. I became intrigued by intellectual property—books, scripts, songs, movies— creations that could provide ongoing income in the form of royalties or residuals. I could be the person who created the product, or I could be the producer who packaged it and took it to market. And with business profits shrinking and the recession beginning, I started looking at these options. The American way—in other words, maintaining significant debt and assuming you'll be fine as long as you invest and have a 401(k)—seemed to be failing the American people, including me.

And so Arthur Wylie, successful wealth management consultant and sought-after public speaker, got fearless and crazy once more and jumped into something new: movies. (For a closer look at all that I do, visit www.arthurwylie.com.)

One of my chief film inspirations was producer/director/ writer James Cameron. His movies have been some of the biggest box-office hits in history. He's the most fearless risk taker in Hollywood. He's a powerful creative force and a technological genius. (You'll read more about him in Chapter 7.) If I wanted to aspire to true greatness in the film business, Cameron was the ideal role model.

Two other filmmakers who also have inspired me are Steven Spielberg, perhaps the greatest cinematic storyteller ever, and Tyler Perry, an ambitious entrepreneur who parlayed his popular stage plays into a film franchise. Perry's movies are often similar, but he knows his audience and what it wants.

Like Perry with his plays, Cameron and Spielberg frequently have taken an asset-backed property, such as a book or play, with a significant audience already "attached," and created hugely successful films. Cameron's *Titanic* and Spielberg's *The Color Purple* are good examples.

I had just the client to get me started on a trajectory similar to that of Cameron, Spielberg, and Perry: *New York Times* best-selling author Omar Tyree.

Tyree's novels have been read by more than 8 million people. He's at 18 books and counting, and in 2001, his *For the Love of Money* won the NAACP Image Award for Outstanding Literary Work, Fiction. In 2006, he won the Phillis Wheatley Literary Award for Body of Work in Urban Fiction. He's a journalist, performance poet, songwriter, screenwriter, entrepreneur, creative genius, and an accomplished public speaker. His books are urban and contemporary but optimistic and uplifting as well. The key was that I knew I could adapt his stories to please a variety of new audiences, across racial and gender lines, who were not his usual fan base but who would still love the topics. His themes are universal: love, friendships, life goal, and lifes challenges.

And he was curious about me and my movie ideas.

Long story short, I have acquired film rights to Tyree's
books and am currently adapting *Leslie*, his supernatural
thriller set in New Orleans, and his best seller, *Flyy Girl*.
Omar Tyree and I became business partners. He creates content, and I leverage that content, find investors and capital,
and look for ways to market his work internationally. I then
form production deals with some of the hottest producers
and writers in Hollywood to balance and expand our creative portfolio. So far, I've struck deals with those responsible
for *The Lord of the Rings, 300, Superman Returns*, and *Final
Destination*.

And we planned on producing some of our new projects at
Wylie Studios in Allen Park, Michigan, outside Detroit. My
fearless and crazy moments seemed to be coming together.

But enough about me (for now). This book is about fearless
and crazy decisions, be they in business or life. We'll look
at some famous ones; we'll look at some simple ones. We'll
discover how those decisions came about and why they worked
(or sometimes didn't). We'll learn how success and failure
often turn on those outrageous, outlandish, from-the-gut
choices. The people in this book, everyone from independent
entrepreneurs and corporate billionaires to a controversial
president and a beloved pope, pulled off tremendous feats
in their chosen fields, reaping phenomenal, unprecedented
rewards despite—or because of—the very real risks.

Most important, we'll get *your* creative juices flowing, get
you thinking about when you've been fearless and crazy and

when you've held back and waited. We'll give you insights and tips to help you prepare yourself for the unexpected, the surprising, and the unique. We'll get you ready to make that split-second call, to take that leap of faith, or to follow that gut instinct—just like all the men and women in this book did.

So strap yourself in. It's going to get crazy.

ONLY THE CRAZY AND FEARLESS

WIN BIG!

1

SETTING THE STAGE

Good fortune is what happens when opportunity meets with planning.

—THOMAS A. EDISON

Before we get to our featured men, women, and corporations, I need to give you the context—provide you the overview for the lessons and inspirations you'll take away from these pages. Everything you're about to read and (I hope) enjoy fits nicely under an umbrella I call my *life-wealth* plan. It's a prescription, a blueprint, for success both professionally and personally. All the true tales in the coming chapters contain elements of the plan. One way or another, the fearless and crazy choices, the life-altering decisions, the incredible business instincts, and the flat-out entrepreneurial genius demonstrated by the people profiled here reflect the life-wealth plan.

What exactly is life-wealth? Life-wealth goes beyond money. It is a physical and mental state. It's a powerful feeling of personal satisfaction for today and a confidence in the constant improvement in your life, career, and wealth for tomorrow. It's believing that success and accomplishment are yours, if not right now, soon. It's living a life that is wealthy in every way. People talk a lot about fulfilling their dreams. Personally, I don't like reaching for dreams; dreams are for sleepers. I want people to achieve *life-wealth*, which is a higher state of accomplishment than mere dreams and wishful thinking. Life-wealth is real, tangible.

The following are life-wealth's components, in strategic order:

- Vision
- Planning
- Execution
- Marketing
- Networking
- Dealing with the Unknown

Let's take a brief look at each of these before you see them in action in the stories you are about to read.

Vision

What is vision? The best definition is *a manifestation of something yet to come.* That's right, something that hasn't happened—yet! Successful entrepreneurs don't just try to make something happen, or hope that it will happen, or dream about something happening, or have illusions that it has happened. No, successful entrepreneurs *do* it. They take that vision and make it reality. The following are some further insights about the vision component of life-wealth:

- The first step on the road to change is a clear and profound impression of what you want—that is, a vision of where you want the future to take you.
- Visions can be crazy. In fact, it's often an advantage to see a crazy future for yourself. It may very well direct you toward possibilities you couldn't otherwise imagine. Having a crazy future in mind will also help motivate you to be fearless in the choices you make down the road.
- Be specific about what you visualize, however. Even crazy visions need to be properly processed, so don't forget to take the time to think practically about what that vision means, what practical steps you have to take in your life to make it a reality, and how it will affect your life goals. For example, if you want to start your own business and set your own hours, establish precisely what kind of business you want to be involved in and how you want your time to be structured.

So how do you make your vision reality? Well, you begin
by moving on to the next component of life-wealth.

4

Planning

The late Norman Vincent Peale, author of *The Power of Positive Thinking*, once said, "Plan your work for today and every day, then work your plan."

There are several dimensions to fearless and crazy planning:

- → Thoroughly evaluate the resources you have at your disposal to transform your vision into a reality.
- → Make a detailed assessment of what you really want for yourself, based on your mission and purpose.
- → Align your resources and ambitions to establish the right direction for your efforts.
- → Ensure that you maintain the right balance of focus and flexibility in your planning.
- → Establish a clear time frame for accomplishing your goals. Short-, mid-, and long-term planning are essential for developing your goals in a strategic, yet fearless and crazy format. Because of your well-thought-out plan, you are able to take quick, appropriate actions when the situations and opportunities fit that plan neatly and nicely. You are ready—and you strike. As you'll see over and over in the pages that follow, fearless and crazy only works when there is a plan in place. Observers may think you're out of your mind, but you had your mind made up long ago—you planned.

A natural outgrowth of planning is developing a mission statement that will inspire you to act and follow through on   5 your plan even when the situation seems relatively hopeless or simply unappealing.

What next? Now it's time to work the plan, to execute.

Execution

I'm a believer in making realistic dreams come true—in other words, *executing the achievable.*

Does this mean I sell my dreams short? Not for one second.

Instead, it means I work harder to ensure that I'm shooting for the right goals at the right time. It means I do my due diligence to guarantee success, rather than just rushing into an opportunity blind with no preparation or realistic potential for success.

Plan big—and execute even bigger!

The following points about execution are worth knowing:

- Execution is one of the hardest phases in any development project.
- You choose whether to react positively or negatively to every situation that comes at you. Obstacles should be treated as action verbs—that is, as opportunities to take action in the pursuit of your goals.
- Motivating people to follow through on their plans is incredibly difficult; don't be surprised if you struggle with this throughout your career. Leading by example, however, is one of the best execution strategies you can

6

embrace. You'll inspire others to follow through on their plans as well.

➡ Execution is as much about reacting to change as it is about following a plan. You have to be rational (for the most part), and your response should be considered (which is where the planning tends to come in), but you also have to be ready to act decisively.

➡ Keep your vision and your plan in the forefront of your mind always. Write down your short-term goals, and revise them daily as you accomplish some and reconsider others. Review your mid- and long-term goals at least monthly. These lists are part of your *daily* routine. You see them before you shut off the light at night; you see them when you wake up each morning. These goals become an integral part of your being. You are never far away from them; nor are they far from you. They are your execution road map. They are the blueprint to the life of your dreams.

We never act in a vacuum, of course. So to execute any plan, to sell any product or service, it's crucial that you sell yourself. This is where marketing comes in.

Marketing

Marketing is what will allow you to rise above the clutter, to distinguish yourself from the masses, to make a mark with your very special vision. It's how you develop your brand.

In fact, that brand is *you*, and marketing is how you develop *Product You.*

You begin developing Product You by figuring out how you are going to be different and why anyone would choose you over the numerous other people offering similar products or services. Basically, what will attract people to you and your business?

Why will they look for *you*, and how will they find you? In traditional marketing and advertising, we call this the *unique selling proposition.* Your unique selling proposition will allow you to establish yourself as a brand in your career or industry and maximize your overall potential. Most companies apply marketing tools and techniques on a day-to-day basis, but individuals rarely see themselves as a "product" or employ marketing tools and techniques to promote and merchandise themselves. Here are some reasons you must develop a marketing strategy for Product You and some tips on how to get started:

- The success of your business depends a great deal on the image you create for your company and your brand.
- A huge part of your business image is determined by your communications and interactions with customers.
- You, yourself, are a brand as well, distinct from any company you are involved with, and marketing yourself successfully is as fundamental to your business success as the marketing of that company. We'll learn much more about brands in Chapter 3.
- When it comes to promoting your business venture and yourself, you need to establish a short, sharp, and

8

effective method to communicate the key marketing message. Work on it, practice it, and perfect it. (See more on this "power statement" in the next section.)

➡ A SWOT analysis is one of the best ways of evaluating your resources and, most important, yourself. It's a great tool for discovering and marketing Product You. You'll learn more about it in Chapter 8 and try it for yourself in Chapter 10.

So now you're concentrating on your image and your brand, but you have to constantly be attuned to others—how they can help you attain your vision and how you can help them achieve theirs.

Networking

I call it *no-nonsense networking*—the ability to work with and through other people who will elevate *your* vision and at the same time promote theirs as well. As a result, you will both add value to one another. You don't network effectively if you're forever thinking only, *What can this person do for me?*

No-nonsense networking is a win-win—if not immediately, then sometime in the future. To get the most out of no-nonsense networking, you have to figure out how to develop a business relationship with people you've met even casually. That may involve something as simple as sending a follow-up email after meeting a person for the first time.

Easy enough? Hardly. For most of us, it's tough being Mr.

or Ms. Social. It's difficult to walk up to strangers, put out your hand, and strike up a conversation. Chitchatting and keeping on top of the relevant topics is not effortless when you're worried about how you look, how you sound, and what to say. Let's face it, we're self-conscious animals, and paying attention to some other self goes against our nature.

But you do it anyway. Because that's how relationships are formed, partnerships are struck, and friendships are begun. It's how business gets done. So if you're not good at it, you'll have to get a bit fearless and crazy just to acquire the skills, just to become at ease. But do it. Persist. It is crucial to everything in this game we call life.

Enough philosophizing. Social scientists who study business interactions say you have about 20 seconds to make a strong, positive impression when meeting someone. If that's true—and it probably is, although 20 seconds may actually be 10 seconds too many—you should prepare what I call a *power statement* for face-to-face business meetings and even chance encounters. Some call it an "elevator speech." Whatever you call it, it should be short, direct, and to the point.

I call my own power statement *20 Seconds of Thunder.* When I'm getting ready to leave the house for another long day of networking, wheeling and dealing, and producing a feature motion picture, I don't walk out the front door unless I have two things: my laptop and my 20 Seconds of Thunder!

So if I run into someone who might help me in the elevator, in the coffee shop, in the lobby, in the reception area, or in the men's room (hey, it has happened) and he casually says, "Oh yeah, Arthur, what are you working on?" I am prepared to the nth degree. I don't stammer and stutter and choke. I don't hand him a business card and tell him to call me sometime. I come ready with my 20 Seconds of Thunder. I tell him in that brief amount of time exactly what I'm working on, who's involved, and how far along we are in the process. People typically respond well because the statement is so succinct. It immediately conveys professionalism, sincerity, and trust. It's no-nonsense.

The following are my seven essential steps to no-nonsense networking:

1. Have a plan and a goal for your networking activities and efforts.
2. Prepare a "script," and practice what you're going to say.
3. Get involved with and engage the person you're meeting.
4. Focus on building the relationship, not making the sale.
5. Don't forget to ask for what you want.
6. Follow up meetings within 24 to 48 hours.
7. Most important, relax and have fun.

We'll explore networking strategy further in Chapter 6.

Life-wealth and its components should be making some sense to you by now. For more about it and to offer your comments, visit www.crazyandfearless.com. There's logic and even a bit of the obvious to life-wealth. But it's never easy—there are always curveballs, blind sides, and surprises.

Dealing with the Unknown

Many people never succeed because they're afraid to try. Rather than make the attempt—and accept the risk of surprises and failure—they don't even step up to the plate. They simply shrug their shoulders, shake their heads, and say they're being realistic.

The power of a fearless and crazy persona is that it makes you that much more ready for the surprises because you have been responsible for a few surprises of your own along the way. Fearless and crazy means ready and willing. Bring it on, whatever it is.

Yes, it's the unknown, and it's unnerving and even scary. But that doesn't mean you can't be ready for it. Here's how:

- Have backup plans. They're crucial. Always have a plan B and even a C and a D.
- Be vigilant and adaptable. Be ready to go with the flow if you have to.
- If you don't have a strong foundation in finances, get one. Or find someone who has one. We're primarily talking about business here, so never neglect the numbers and what they mean. That financial knowledge can make your backup that much stronger.
- Practice makes perfect. The more times you have to react to and deal with the unknown, the better you get at it. Just about every person and company profiled in this book has had plenty of practice.

Sure, you may fail, take your lumps, find yourself bruised, and even lose a game or two. But at least you were in the game. Life is a state of constant change, so don't live your life in a state of constant *standstill.*

If the unknown wins this time, shake it off, smile, and go to plan B. Be fearless and crazy, and come back for more.

That's what the people in this book did.

2

THE ELEMENT OF SURPRISE

A man surprised is half beaten.

—THOMAS FULLER

By definition, a fearless and crazy decision has an element of surprise. It's the unexpected, the shake-your-head, drop-your-jaw, where-did-that-come-from memorable moment. History and life—yours included—have these moments. What's important is recognizing them when you see them, learning from them, and applying them to your personal and professional life. The element of surprise can give you that decided advantage and make you the victor when all seems lost. The following three surprising tales illustrate this.

14   An End Around

It was midsummer 1950. The United Nations forces had held the line, but the situation was getting more desperate by the day. It had all begun on June 25, when troops of the Communist Democratic People's Republic of Korea (North Korea) swept across the 38th parallel into the Western-aligned Republic of Korea (South Korea). The North Korean soldiers advanced swiftly and brutally, taking Seoul, the South Korean capital, and pushing the South Korean army down the peninsula.

The UN Security Council passed Resolution 82 authorizing the United Nations to send armed forces to assist the hapless South Koreans. The United States was empowered to appoint the UN commander, and the U.S. Joint Chiefs of Staff unanimously chose General Douglas MacArthur, World War II hero of the Pacific, Medal of Honor winner, and one of the most famous military men in American history.

The perfect choice for a tough job.

From his headquarters in Japan, MacArthur took command of South Korea's army and on July 1 received permission to commit U.S. forces as well. The American troops were hastily assembled and poorly equipped. They entered the fray and did all they could to slow the North Korean onslaught. But the Communists pushed on, finally surrounding the UN forces at Pusan in the extreme southeast corner of the Korean Peninsula. The UN soldiers held—for now—setting up a line that would be known in history as the Pusan Perimeter. They

would either continue to hold that line or be pushed into the
sea, allowing South Korea to fall.

Throughout August 1950 the fighting and dying around
Pusan continued. And General MacArthur worked on his
fearless and crazy plan to turn the tide. He gathered his top
generals and admirals in his Tokyo office and laid out his
scheme. Never one to practice humility, he compared what
he was proposing to British general James Wolfe's strategy at
the Battle of the Plains of Abraham (also known as the Battle
of Quebec) in the French and Indian War. In a risky surprise
move, Wolfe had sent troops by boat upriver past the French
lines to slip ashore, scale the cliffs, and outflank the enemy
and cut their supply lines. The maneuver succeeded, and the
battle was won.

But now in the summer of 1950, MacArthur had some
persuading to do.

The city of Inchon, in the far northwest corner of South
Korea, just below the 38th parallel, was far from the Pusan
Perimeter. Because it was so far from hostilities, the city
was only lightly defended by the occupying North Koreans.
Inchon was MacArthur's target.

His plan was simple and complicated at the same time. He
would send an amphibious force from Pusan around the peninsula and up to Inchon. Marines and Army troops would
land on the rocky shore, scale the surrounding seawalls, and
take the city, thereby outflanking the enemy and cutting off
their supply lines—just like Wolfe at Quebec. From Inchon,
the UN troops could quickly sweep toward Seoul, only about
20 miles away, and turn the course of the war.

Simple? Hardly. First of all, the Marines, who would be key to the surprise assault, had been significantly drawn down in the five years since the end of World War II. What was left of the force would have to be hastily regrouped and reequipped.

Nature and geography would also be problems. Approaches to the city from the water consisted of just two narrow channels, passages that could easily be mined. Also, the current in the channels was dangerously swift—three to eight knots. Finally, the anchorage was small, and the harbor below the city was surrounded by tall seawalls (just like the cliffs fronting Wolfe's Quebec). Said Navy commander Arlie Capps, "We drew up a list of every natural and geographic handicap— and Inchon had 'em all."[1]

MacArthur's officers argued, protested, and even suggested alternative sites. But MacArthur was not to be dissuaded. He adjusted and revised some of the details, but the target remained Inchon. He argued that because of all the city's natural defenses, the North Koreans would not expect an attack there; victory at Inchon would avoid a costly winter campaign to push out from Pusan; taking Inchon would cut off enemy lines of communication; and, most important, Inchon was not far from Seoul, the ultimate target and the linchpin of the war.

"I can almost hear the ticking of the second hand of destiny," said MacArthur to his commanders. "We must act now

---

1 Edward J. Marolda, *The U.S. Navy in the Korean War* (Annapolis, MD: Naval Institute Press, 207), 68.

or we will die. . . . We shall land at Inchon, and I shall crush them."[2]

MacArthur code-named the Inchon assault Operation Chromite. His superiors in Washington, D.C., approved the plan. Soon the world would know just how fearless and crazy it was.

In preparation for the assault, the UN forces sent in spies to learn more about the city's fortifications and the harbor's tides, mudflats, and seawalls. The United Nations also sent Air Force bombers to soften up the city and surroundings. UN troops even conducted a few practice landings at coastal sites similar to Inchon. The North Koreans considered all this a mere nuisance, minor distractions from the standoff at Pusan.

In the five days before the scheduled September 15 landing, warships from the United States and Canada bombarded Inchon and its harbor, primarily targeting gun emplacements. Finally, the North Koreans realized something big might just be coming. But it was much too late to do anything about it. At 6:30 A.M. on September 15, 1950, the first tank landing ships (LSTs) of the UN attack force pushed ashore on one of the Inchon beaches. The landing force was made up of Marines and an Army tank battalion. The second wave came ashore that evening at two other nearby beaches. The North Korean forces, outnumbered six to one, resisted fiercely but

---

2 Leatherneck Guide Inc, Leatherneck.com, Reference Section, History and Museum Division, http://www.leatherneck.com/forums/archive/index.php/t-6370.html.

had to give ground. It was all over in just five days, with UN troops firmly in control of the harbor and the city. Supplies and reinforcements streamed ashore.

General MacArthur watched the initial assault of September 15 from the bridge of the USS *Mount McKinley* just outside the harbor. On September 17 he visited the battlefield itself, inspecting the wreckage of six North Korean tanks that had been knocked out by the Marines. As he walked around the burned-out tank hulls, North Korean sniper fire rang out. MacArthur simply continued his inspection tour, noting that the North Korean marksmen were poorly trained.

Operation Chromite—the surprise amphibious assault at Inchon—had been an unqualified success. It would go down in military history and lore as one of the greatest strategic moves ever, even more impressive than Wolfe's at Quebec.

Yet the momentum of the victory was squandered. The "sweep" on to Seoul turned out to be a slow, bloody slog. Eventually, UN troops broke out from Pusan and advanced north. Seoul fell, and thousands of North Korean troops retreated back across the 38th parallel, with the UN allies in pursuit. The People's Republic of China warned the United Nations not to push on all the way to the Yalu River, the Chinese border. MacArthur dismissed the Chinese threat as empty, but on November 25, 1950, the People's Republic of China sent thousands of its soldiers across the river into North Korea. The overwhelming Chinese force pushed the UN Allies back down past the 38th parallel in disarray.

In early 1951, the Allies regrouped, recaptured Seoul, and advanced again toward the parallel. MacArthur wanted

to push on, of course, and continued to criticize his superiors, including President Truman, for their timid, limited
war strategy. He also publicly threatened to attack China if
there was no quick truce. Truman had had enough; he fired
MacArthur on April 11, 1951, for "insubordination."[3]

Fighting on the Korean Peninsula continued for another
two years, ending with a stalemate and a truce in July 1953.
That truce remains in force to this day. North and South
Korea are still officially at war.

As for Inchon, today it is a bustling city of 2.8 million and
a transportation hub featuring that famous harbor as well
as South Korea's main international airport. It also boasts
Korea's tallest building. Yet its name will always trigger mem-
ories and images of a bigger-than-life general and his fearless
plan of attack so many decades ago.

Half Off

Some people—and companies—are full of surprises. They
never cease to amaze us with their words and actions. They
raise eyebrows; they get heads shaking.

And sometimes their surprises command our admiration
and respect.

Such is the case with Groupon, the hugely successful
online coupon and gift certificate provider that has become

---

3 "Relieving MacArthur of His Command," Foundation of the National Ar-
chives, 11 April 1951, http://www.digitalvaults.org/record/3392.html.

a household word in the few short years since its November 2008 launch.

There's nothing complicated about the basic Groupon service. The name itself is simple—a combination of "group" and "coupon." When you sign up, you receive an email offer once a day for a retailer or service in your area, or sometimes for a national store. Most of the deals run from 50 percent off to 90 percent off. You have a time limit (usually several hours) in which to sign up, and there is a set number of Groupons available for each offer. These restrictions keep participating retailers from being overrun by Groupon-clutching customers. In addition, the coupon has to be redeemed within a certain period of time, usually several months.

For example, let's say today's Groupon is for $40 of food and drink at a local sports bar for the price of $20. Half off. You sign up (before the expiration), pay your $20 via credit card or PayPal, print out your Groupon, and use it at the restaurant sometime before the end date. You'll get $40 worth of food and drink for your $20 advance payment. That $20 is split, usually 50-50, between the sports bar and Groupon. Sure, the retailer is offering a deep discount, but it is also getting added business and good marketing buzz.

The simple plan was the brainchild of Groupon CEO and founder Andrew Mason, who in the fall of 2008 began offering half-price pizzas online from the first-floor restaurant of his Chicago office building. Mason convinced his former employer, Eric Lefkofsky, to invest $1 million in his "group coupon" idea, and as they say, the rest is history. Three years later Mason's booming enterprise was "on pace to make $1 billion in sales faster than any other business, ever," according to *Forbes*.[4]

People like bargains, and they like Groupon's user-friendly way to get those bargains: an email a day. If you like it, buy it. If not, delete. The service offers more than a thousand daily deals to 83 million subscribers in 43 countries. It employs more than 7,100 workers. But the ink is still red. In 2010, Groupon brought in revenue of $713 million but still lost a net of $413 million when expenses were factored in. Yet it's that unprecedented revenue growth, racing toward $1 billion, that has gotten everyone's attention.

At its core, Groupon is just a clever online method to market a traditional service; after all, coupons are as old as the corner grocery store. Even online coupon websites have been around since the tech bubble days of the 1990s. And Groupon isn't the first high-profile online enterprise to attract celebrity-like attention and through-the-roof revenue projections. Facebook, eBay, and LinkedIn come to mind. So what is it about Groupon that makes us smile, aside from a good deal on a massage treatment? Where are the Groupon surprises?

To begin with, Groupon and Mason, still only in his early thirties, turned down a couple of amazing buyout offers in late 2010. Throughout that year, the company's *monthly* revenues grew from $11 million to $89 million. The big boys were noticing. In October 2010, rumors had Yahoo! offering

4 Christopher Steiner, "Meet the Fastest Growing Company Ever," *Forbes* magazine, August 30, 2010, http://www.forbes.com/forbes/2010/0830/entrepreneurs-groupon-facebook-twitter-next-web-phenom.html.

$3 billion to acquire the company. On November 30, 2010, Google came calling, publicly offering $6 billion.

Mason and his investors didn't think about it for very long. After a few days, on December 3, 2010, they said thanks-but-no-thanks. With characteristic nonchalance they turned down one of the largest buyout offers in history.

Instead, the company spent the following few weeks attracting more private investment in the company and building a considerable cash stockpile, thereby positioning itself for its initial public offering (IPO) in the fall of 2011. Groupon had decided to go public the old-fashioned way and let the investors finance its future and determine its worth. Those private investors who came on board before the IPO would do very well as Groupon stock went on the market.

Mason's June 2011 IPO filing was anything but traditional. Again he raised eyebrows with his irreverent wit and fresh-faced charm. In his cover letter accompanying the filing, Mason revealed his business philosophy with a simple statement: "Life is too short to be a boring company." He warned that his about-to-be-public company will have "twists and turns, moments of brilliance and other moments of sheer stupidity." Groupon's goal, he wrote, is to "create experiences for our customers that make today different enough from yesterday to justify getting out of bed."[5]

Other Groupon surprises—some of them worth getting out of bed for—include the following:

---

5 "Read Groupon CEO's Letter to IPO Investors, "CNNMoney, June 2, 2011, http://money.cnn.com/2011/06/02/technology/Groupon_CEO_shareholder_letter/index.htm?iid=EL.

- The company is picky about the retailers, restaurants, and services it partners with to offer deals. It doesn't take just anybody, even though virtually everybody is ready to jump on the Groupon bandwagon. In fact, Groupon rejects seven out of eight possible deals suggested by retailers. It will not work with shooting ranges, abortion clinics, plastic surgeons, and strip clubs.

23

- CEO Mason's annual salary is a mere $575 (but he does own 23 million shares of Groupon stock).
- Groupon shares the wealth. It "pays" consumers and companies to spread the word and drive business to Groupon. Not only does it pay $10 in Groupon credits for each additional person a member convinces to sign up for the service, but it also offers an "affiliate" program to businesses. Those that include a geo-targeted Groupon smart link (widget) on their company website earn as much as 15 percent commission on all Groupon deals generated through them.
- Groupon daily discounts are with local, mostly small businesses. That's the backbone of the company's strategy. You buy the deal because it's for your local downtown bistro or your mall fitness center. But in August 2010 Groupon offered a national deal, partnering with giant retailer Gap. As always, the discount was simple: $50 in Gap clothing or accessories for $25. The coupons sold at a rate of 10 per second, meaning 200,000 of the deal vouchers sold before noon on the day of the launch. The response overwhelmed the company's computer servers even though it had boosted capacity in anticipation of a successful launch. National deals will be part of the Groupon mix going forward.

- The company has partnered with online travel giant Expedia to bring deep discounts to leisure and business travelers. The partnership and Groupon's simple buying procedure have the potential to knock the entire world-wide travel industry on its ear. Stay tuned.

- In spring 2011, the company launched Grouspawn, described by Mason as "a foundation we created that awards college scholarships to babies whose parents used a Groupon on their first date."[6] Get it? Grou-*spawn*. The company and Mason are serious; the details of the initiative are laid out on its website (grouspawn.com), with FAQs outlining such puzzles as how the Groupon-using couple will prove that their particular spawn session occurred after their Groupon date.

- The company has developed a mobile app called Groupon Now! that it is testing in several large cities. The app allows Groupon members to find a discount for a specific participating merchant immediately when they are near that merchant's location. The instant deal will pop up as a message on the member's smart phone. No more waiting for a daily email.

After a series of revenue restatements, Groupon finally went public on November 4, 2011, raising $700 million, the most successful Internet company IPO since Google Inc. raised $1.7 billion in 2004. For CEO Mason the result was just the latest in the long line of Groupon surprises. As he

---

6 Ibid.

had advised (warned?) prospective investors: "Expect us to make ambitious bets on our future that distract us from our current business."[7] 25

On the Ropes

In October 1974, the champ's best years seemed to be behind him. In fact, he was the *former* heavyweight champion of the world. The last few years of his storied career were anything but impressive. He had lost a brutal "Fight of the Century" to then-champion Joe Frazier in March 1971, just three and a half years earlier. It was his first professional loss. Then in 1973, he fought Ken Norton, suffering a broken jaw even as he won a 12-round split decision. Later that year he won a rematch with Norton, also by split decision. That earned him a rematch with Frazier, who had recently lost his title. Although he beat Frazier on January 28, 1974, in a unanimous 12-round decision, it had not been a stellar last few years. He was tired. He was 32 years old.

Now it was October, and he was getting another title shot. He was about to fight George Foreman—the popular George Foreman who had won a gold medal for the United States at the 1968 Olympics in Mexico City. The George Foreman who had knocked out both Frazier and Norton in two rounds. The George Foreman who in that title fight with Frazier had knocked the champ down six times in the bout's

---

7 Ibid.

first 4 minutes and 25 seconds. The George Foreman who
26   was the heavyweight champion of the world. The George
Foreman who at 25 was at the peak of his power.

And he would fight Foreman in Kinshasa, Zaire. They
were billing it as "The Rumble in the Jungle."

To Muhammad Ali, it would be that and more.

He and Foreman had spent the summer of 1974 training
in Zaire so that their bodies would be completely accli-
mated to the hot, humid weather. Throughout those lead-
in weeks and months, Ali met frequently with the press and
endeared himself to the local population. He was a natural
self-promoter, of course, but he was also pro-African and
frequently said so.

He boasted again and again how he was too fast for
Foreman and would come out immediately in the first
round with a flurry of punches and dazzling footwork—an
aggressive strategy. But with a sly smile, he would also men-
tion he had a "secret plan" to take out the defending champ.
Foreman, meanwhile, trained mostly in seclusion, quiet and
confident, although he and his trainers were well aware of
what Ali was saying.

As the October 30 fight drew near, celebrities and fight
fans from across the globe descended on Kinshasa. For three
nights preceding the bout, a music festival called Zaire '74
treated the crowds to a long list of entertainers, including
James Brown, B. B. King, and Miriam Makeba. The city had
become a circus.

But now it was time to put the gloves on.

Later, in the days and weeks after the fight, Foreman, author

Norman Mailer and several others all claimed they saw Ali's handlers loosen the ring's ropes in the hours before the opening bell.[8] Maybe. But there was still a battle to be won or lost.

Round 1 went the way Ali had said it would, with him the fleet-footed aggressor. But he uncharacteristically often led with his right, tempting fate if one of Foreman's powerful punches landed. Ali backpedaled and sideswiped as he punched, but by round's end, Foreman was effectively cutting off the ring and scoring with a few shots of his own. Time for the secret plan.

In round 2, Foreman expected a toe-to-toe slugfest, but instead Ali leaned back into the ropes time and time again, letting Foreman flail away at him. He'd taunt Foreman, lean back and protect only his face. Foreman's body punches lost much of their power as the ropes gave way to the leaning Ali. Also, Ali would move his head and body in perfect timing, making many of Foreman's blows glancing or outright misses. And as he did so, Ali would snap off a counterpunch or two. Vintage Muhammad Ali.

Ali continued with his retreat-to-the-ropes strategy for the next several rounds, as the frustrated, angry Foreman swung again and again. Occasionally, Ali would dart away and land a few combinations of his own. He took every opportunity to fire straight punches at Foreman's face. But mostly he leaned back against the ropes and weathered the Foreman storm.

---

8 Ron Kurtus, "Strategy Used by Muhammad Ali to Beat George Foreman in 1974," 2007, school-for-champions.com, http://www.school-for-champions.com/competition/boxing_ali_foreman.htm.

And, not surprisingly, he kept up the chatter: "They told me you could punch, George! They told me you could punch as hard as Joe Louis!"

By round 7, Foreman was punched out. His tired arms all but hung at his sides. Ali then turned on his speed and energy and began scoring points. Foreman simply tried for a knockout punch.

"Is that all you got, George?" taunted Ali, after the desperate champ managed to land a punishing body blow.

"Yup, that's about it," answered Foreman.[9]

It ended in the eighth round with a five-punch combination from Ali, followed by a left hook that brought Foreman's head up and then a straight right to the face that sent him tumbling to the canvas. Foreman managed to struggle to his feet, but not before the referee had counted him out.

Muhammad Ali was Heavyweight Champion of the World once more.

And Ali's fearless and crazy secret plan—what he immediately after the fight called "rope-a-dope"—became boxing legend. In fact, today the term *rope-a-dope* is frequently used to describe a strategy in which one person pretends to be losing, hoping to lure a stronger opponent into overextending himself and setting him up for defeat. Politicians, businessmen, and soldiers often employ the term to describe their plans for success. But rope-a-dope will always belong to the magnificent Ali—and the powerful Foreman.

Ultimately, the two fighters became friends. When the

---

9 "The Rumble in the Jungle," Wikipedia.org, March 31, 2011, http://en.wikipedia.org/wiki/The_Rumble_in_the_Jungle.

1996 documentary about the classic fight, *When We Were Kings*, won an Oscar, George Foreman helped the Parkinson's-suffering Ali up the stairs to receive the award along with the filmmakers.

■ ■ ■

⇒ MY TAKE

"I *hate* surprises!" You've most likely heard that line before—from a boss, a business partner, a friend, or even a spouse. Maybe you've said it yourself a time or two. And we all know what it means. We don't like to be thrown out of our comfort zones. We don't want to have to react—make the call, turn on a dime, yes or no, thumbs up or down, fight or flight—without having time to think and consider. Without having time to make one of those pros-and-cons lists. Quick decisions are rarely good decisions. Our brains are built to mull over things, to weigh possibilities, to ponder outcomes. No surprises!

And all of that is mostly true for your own business, your own career, and your own family. But when it comes to dealing with the competition, the element of surprise is a wonderful tool. It gives you the advantage. It suddenly gives you control. You become master of the situation. Your competition—be it in a boardroom, on a battlefield, or in a stadium—is forced to scramble, adjust, and react. Because your competition hates surprises. The North Koreans, George Foreman, and all those online coupon websites hated surprises. But the surprises—fearless and crazy as they were—prevailed.

Remember, it's a surprise to the competition, but to you

30

it's carefully thought out, thoroughly planned, and perfectly executed. MacArthur, the folks at Groupon, and Ali knew just what they were doing from start to finish. Their masterful plans sent their competition into disarray and defeat.

As an entrepreneur (or a soon-to-be entrepreneur) you look for ways to surprise your rivals, to gain an unexpected advantage in the marketplace. Maybe it's a new product you suddenly launch. Maybe it's a special person you suddenly hire. Maybe it's a building you buy, a place you relocate to, or an investment you make. Just when they think they've got you figured out, you zing them. Fearless and crazy. But planned all along. It's a key element in the life-wealth strategy outlined in Chapter 1. It's *planning*—with power.

All right, so you're always looking for ways to spring a surprise. Maybe you even brainstorm possible surprises with your coworkers, write them down, and get them ready to go. But then you've got to do it. You've got to pull the trigger, push the button, sign the order, give the nod, just say yes.

MacArthur did it. Groupon's Andrew Mason did it. Ali did it.

When he was deciding to run for president in 2007, Barack Obama used a phrase I just love: "the fierce urgency of now." He wasn't going to wait. Many in the political game said he was too young, too inexperienced. But he said no. The time is now.

As one of my buddies, film producer and entrepreneur Louis Lautman, puts it, "If you asked me the best time to start, I would tell you *right now*. If you asked me six months from right now, I would give you the same answer: *Do it now, do it now, do it now.*" To be more specific, put together your plan of attack now, and be ready to execute that plan when- ever and wherever it feels right. Don't just rush onto the bat- tlefield because the time is *now* and end up getting your arm broken or your head blown off. Rush in *prepared*. Because you've planned; you're ready. Remember, it is battle.

That said, action is absolutely fundamental—whatever it is you're aiming to do, whatever surprise you've got in mind. You've done the planning, now you *execute* that plan—again, a key life-wealth component.

Anyone can talk a big game, dress to the nines, drive a fancy car, or say he's "committed to the project," but when it comes down to brass tacks, most people fold rather than execute. It has been true in my experience, and it will be in yours.

Many times I thought I had a new source of funding locked down, but an investor backed out.

Many times I thought I had an actor lined up, but he took another job.

Many times I thought I had the script nailed down tight, but someone, somewhere, wanted another rewrite.

Many times I thought I had the perfect location for shooting a particular scene all set up, but something hap- pened and I had to scramble to find a new perfect spot.

In fact, the more people you get involved in a project, the more potential there is for things to go wrong. In my life-wealth plan, I call that *dealing with the unknown*. Those unknowns are out there, and they're going to pop up; you just don't know where or when. But you expect them; you're ready for them.

You make sure the people who work for you and with you

32

are also ready and willing to execute the plan, that they are unafraid of the unknowns and surprises. In short, you want people who do what they say and say what they do.

So which type of person are you?

Do you talk a lot and do a little?

Or do you say what you do and do what you say?

I started my film enterprise with a good product: proven best sellers by a respected author, Omar Tyree, who wrote magical and timely stories. I researched the industry and developed a power plan. I built a team and attracted A-list producers. Then I made sure it made sense on paper—that my financials were so solid we could not only get the films produced but also distributed.

Distribution, I realized pretty quickly, was going to be fundamental to the success of my studio. Films have to be seen on the big screen, many big screens, or else they're just hobby projects. Distribution is key. To become a major player in Hollywood, I had to figure out distribution.

So I focused on developing a strong support group of mentors and businesspeople around the project. Those people made my initial run to line up investment capital easier but not easy. With no prior experience and only a few contacts in the film business, this was a challenging task. That reality, combined with the start of a global recession, made this venture one of the toughest I had ever faced.

But I was doing it. I was fearlessly executing my plan. I wasn't wringing my hands; I wasn't waiting just a little while longer. I was making decisions and moving forward—and surprising everyone at every step in my journey.

So many people are focused on what they can't do instead

of taking advantage of what's right there in front of them, the very things they can control. People bump their heads against the same brick wall over and over simply because they're concentrating on the problem instead of seeing the solutions and making them happen.

It sounds easy, but of course, it isn't. Everyone has real-life situations, issues, and problems that can keep him from reaching his goals. Some are insurmountable—if you're five foot four, you're not going to play in the NBA—but many are not. And those are the ones you tackle, finesse, outlast, and defeat. As former football coach Lou Holtz likes to say, "Ten percent of life is what happens to you; 90 percent is how you react to it."

So react. Raise some eyebrows. Attract some criticism.

Or just shake your head, lie back in the recliner, and be a "gonna" person.

A "gonna" person is someone who says:

- "I'm gonna do it, but I'm tired after work."
- "I'm gonna do it, but I'll wait until my kids are old enough."
- "I'm gonna do it right after my next promotion."
- "I'm gonna start saving for my future as soon as I make a little more money."

"Gonna" people are always gonna do something. A "gonna" person always has an excuse, a perfectly logical reason why not—why not *now*, anyway. But they're gonna do it later. As we all know, too often "later" never comes.

So what about you? Gonna? Or not? Surprise us. Or as the folks at Nike say, "Just do it."

3

BRAND NAMES

When people use your brand name as a verb, that is remarkable.

—MEG WHITMAN

Sometimes in business and in life, who people *think* you are is just as important as—and maybe more important than—who you really are. Building a brand—personal, professional, or corporate—is key in a world where marketing and PR often decide success or failure. Individuals, companies, entire cultures and societies respond negatively or positively to that brand. It may seem crass, but build the right brand and you can conquer the world, or at least survive another day.

The following are the stories of three deliberate, well-orchestrated brands.

Like a Virgin

According to data collected by marketing research company BrandZ, the top 10 most valuable brands in the world in 2011 were:

1. Apple
2. Google
3. IBM
4. McDonald's
5. Microsoft
6. Coca-Cola
7. AT&T
8. Marlboro
9. China Mobile
10. GE[10]

Conspicuous by their absence were Amazon, Verizon, Walmart, UPS, Hewlett-Packard, and Visa.

And Virgin. Yes, that Virgin, the hugely successful brand created, nurtured, and dominated by Richard Branson, an entrepreneur celebrity who has become a brand unto himself.

---

10 Millward Brown Optimor, "BrandZ Top 100 Most Valuable Global Brands," http://www.millwardbrown.com/BrandZ/default.aspx.

To be correct, he's *Sir* Richard Charles Nicholas Branson, a British baron, knighted in 2000. His Virgin Group includes more than 400 companies worldwide. He's the 5th richest person in the United Kingdom and the 254th richest in the world. The following are just a few of the companies wearing the Virgin brand past and present. The list also gives an indication of the diversity of Branson's talents and tastes:

- Virgin Records
- Virgin Games
- Virgin Atlantic Airways
- Virgin Holiday
- Virgin Megastore
- Virgin Publishing
- Virgin Radio
- Virgin Vodka
- Virgin Cola
- Virgin Brides
- Virgin Trains
- Virgin Cosmetics
- Virgin Mobile
- Virgin Australia
- Virgin Energy
- Virgin Cars
- Virgin Galactic
- Virgin Money
- Virgin Healthcare
- Virgin Racing

Whew! And that's just *some* of them. Why "Virgin"? Well, back in the early 1970s, when the young Richard was selling records at a discount through the mail and even out of the boot (trunk) of his car, one of his early employees suggested the name for the company because all of them, Richard included, were virgins in the business world.

Branson wouldn't remain one for long, of course. In 1972, he launched Virgin Records and was soon producing albums for the likes of the Sex Pistols and discovering new acts such as Culture Club. Branson sold Virgin Records to EMI in 1992, primarily because he was so busy with other ventures, including his now-famous airline, his mobile phone company, and even his Australian wine company. One of his most fearless and crazy moments was his 1993 decision to get into the railroad business, with his launch of Virgin Trains. The UK railroads were a financial mess and had a deservedly poor reputation for service. Branson jumped in anyway.

And he pressed on, looking for newer, even crazier opportunities. Why? As he explains it, "My interest in life comes from setting myself huge, apparently unachievable challenges and trying to rise above them."[11]

Case in point #1: In 2004, he launched Virgin Galactic, whose name hints at the mission: space flights for members of the public, with tickets priced at something like $200,000. He is working with Microsoft cofounder Paul Allen and visionary engineer Burt Rutan on the ambitious goal to make

11 Richard Branson, *Losing My Virginity: How I've Survived, Had Fun, and Made a Fortune Doing Business My Way* (New York: Three Rivers Press, 1998).

(potential) astronauts of us all. Apparently, the sky is not the limit for Branson.

Case in point #2: In 2006, he launched Virgin Fuels to respond to global warming concerns and to explore alternative fuel sources. Most corporate leaders shy away from environmental controversies, but Branson embraces them and champions new solutions and possibilities. Virgin Fuels is now Virgin Green Fund. The fuels and green initiatives led naturally to Branson's 2007 announcement of the Virgin Earth Challenge, a global science and technology prize of $25 million to the individual or group that submits "a commercially viable design to achieve the net removal of significant volumes of anthropogenic, atmospheric greenhouse gases each year for at least 10 years without countervailing harmful effects."[12] Branson is putting his money where his passions are.

Branson's high-profile lifestyle often eclipses even his famous companies. The shaggy-headed, wide-smiling star seems to be everywhere. He has set a variety of high-speed ocean sailing records. He has crossed the Pacific in a hot-air balloon and even attempted to circumnavigate the globe in a balloon. He has made numerous appearances in TV series and films, often playing himself. He even had his own Fox network reality show called *The Rebel Billionaire: Branson's Quest for the Best*.

His love of the spotlight allows him to shine a bright light on many causes that are important to him. His nonprofit foundation Virgin Unite established the Branson School of

---

12 "Earth Challenge," http://www.virgin.com/subsites/virgincarth/.

Entrepreneurship in South Africa in 2005. He has used his money and notoriety to work for energy solutions, to push for the elimination of nuclear weapons, to support humanitarian initiatives in Kenya and Sudan, and to promote universal access to broadband services. The list of his charitable, political, and environmental interests could nearly match the list of his Virgin companies. Still in his early sixties, he's unlikely to slow down anytime soon.

"For me business is not about wearing suits or keeping stockholders pleased," says Branson. "It's about being true to yourself, your ideas, and focusing on the essentials."[13]

It's about being true to the brand.

Court of Public Opinion

In 1993, it brought the slimy, scary Menendez brothers right into our living rooms. In 1994 and 1995, it was O. J. Simpson, Judge Ito, Johnnie Cochran, and Kato Kaelin. There were hundreds more, of course—the famous, infamous, and unwashed nobodies. Defendants, lawyers, witnesses, bailiffs, judges, and juries. Our living rooms became courtrooms. It was Court TV, and it was a small-screen sensation.

It began just a couple of years before the Menendez trial, in 1991. The cable network was a joint venture owned by Liberty Media, Time Warner, and General Electric (NBC).

---

13 Sir Richard Branson, "The Development of an Entrepreneur," ReviewEssays.com, http://reviewessays.com/print/Sir-Richard-Branson-Development-Entrepreneur/52979.html.

The face of Court TV was law writer Steven Brill. But other familiar TV journalism names also put in stints at the net- 41 work, including Jack Ford, Dan Abrams, Nancy Grace, Cynthia McFadden, Savannah Guthrie, Terry Moran, and Star Jones.

Court TV was dedicated to live trial coverage—almost always homicides—and a variety of other criminal justice programming. Anchors provided analysis. Thanks to Court TV, America had a seat in front of the judge's bench to watch as justice was and wasn't served and to be reminded that *real-life* courtroom proceedings are often far different from those seen in TV drama series and movies.

Brill left the network in 1997; a year later NBC/General Electric sold its share to Time Warner. That same year, the network began running several original and acquired programs in prime time, such as *Homicide: Life on the Street* and *Forensic Files.*

The branding and programming evolution continued. In 2004, Court TV split into two divisions. Daytime trial coverage was branded as Court TV News, and prime-time and weekend programming was branded as Court TV: Seriously Entertaining.

Time Warner bought full control of Court TV in 2006 and began running it as part of the Turner Broadcasting System. And it was the Turner executives who decided it was time for a step-off-the-cliff, fearless-and-crazy rebranding: a whole new name and more.

Yes, Court TV had become something of an institution in the ever-changing, ever-expanding world of cable television entertainment. But the daily courtroom shows on many of the traditional network channels—*The People's Court, Divorce Court, Judge Judy, Judge Hatchett, Judge Maria Lopez, Judge David Young,* and on and on—were capturing much of the buzz and more and more of the eyeballs. Plus, many "real" judges throughout the country were allowing cameras in the courtroom, so America was often getting the inside look on network news and documentary shows. In addition, reality shows of one kind or another were everywhere and were not just a passing fad. They were not only here to stay and capturing growing audience share, they were also relatively inexpensive to produce. TV wasn't what it used to be.

So in 2008, Court TV changed its name to truTV. As such, it bills itself as "television's destination for real-life stories told from an exciting and dramatic first-person perspective and featuring high-stakes, action-packed originals that give viewers access to places and situations they can't normally experience."[14]

Whew. But a look at the lineup tells you what the network means to say. Among truTV's prime-time fan favorites are the original series *Operation Repo, truTV Presents: World's Dumbest . . . , Hardcore Pawn, Lizard Lick Towing, Disorder in the Court, Forensic Files, Las Vegas Jailhouse, Top 20 Most Shocking,* and *Bait Car.*

In other words, it's not just courtrooms anymore. And that, of course, was the plan. Broaden, expand, rebrand—or be lost in the shuffle and slowly fade away. But truTV does not consider itself a reality network; instead it focuses on series that feature real-life situations—not the contests or highly staged

---

14 "About Us," trutv.com, http://www.trutv.com/about/index.html.

events typical of reality shows. Thus the network's tagline: "Not Reality. Actuality." The line between the two is not always clear, however, and truTV has been accused of staging scenes in some of its more popular shows. But even such accusations end up being good PR for the new name and new lineup. 43

The rebranding seems to be working. Viewership is strong and growing. The risk was great: changing a name in such a crowded, chaotic field could easily have led to oblivion. Remember the cable networks America's Talking and the Nostalgia Channel? Me neither.

But TBS and truTV execs were not completely crazy. They did hedge their bets and keep significant courtroom coverage in their programming lineup. In fact, they gave that coverage its own name, In Session, a new brand within the new brand. It runs from 9 A.M. to 3 P.M. each weekday, after which truTV programming kicks in.

In Session continues to provide the same important service as its ancestor, Court TV: It is the only television network to serve as a window into the American justice system. It offers live coverage of criminal and civil trials from around the country, as well as expert analysis from the network's award-winning legal journalists. The network (old name and new) has covered more than 950 trials since its inception.[15]

So we still can watch the wheels of justice turn. A rebranding decision that was fearless and crazy on its surface but strategic and thorough in its execution will keep the gavels pounding— right in our home on our screens and monitors.

---

15 "The Leader in Trial Coverage," trutv.com, http://www.trutv.com/about/insession/index.html.

44 Reinventing the Wheeler

When we think of inventors, we think of men like Thomas Edison and Alexander Graham Bell. When we think of *reinventors*, we should think of Sean Combs, a.k.a. Puff Daddy, a.k.a. P. Diddy, a.k.a. Diddy. What has Sean Combs reinvented? Himself. Again and again.

His list of roles is long: record producer, rapper, actor, fashion designer, TV producer, restaurant owner, fragrance creator, vodka promoter, philanthropist, and business school founder, among others. His career has had more ups and downs than an amusement park roller coaster, and he has earned a few honors and mentions along the way:

- ➡ MTV Music Video Award winner in 1997 and 1998
- ➡ Grammy Award winner in 1998 (twice) and 2004
- ➡ *Fortune* magazine's 40 Richest Under 40 list for 2002
- ➡ Menswear Designer of the Year for 2004
- ➡ *Time* magazines 100 Most Influential People list for 2006
- ➡ NAACP Image Award for Outstanding Actor in a Television Movie, Mini-Series or Dramatic Special (*A Raisin in the Sun*) in 2009

But things didn't start out too well for Sean Combs. He was born in a public housing project in Harlem and grew up in Mount Vernon, New York. When he was just a boy, his 33-year-old father was shot and killed in his car outside a Manhattan party.

Sean graduated from Mount Saint Michael Academy in

1987. It was there that he earned the nickname "Puff" because he would huff and puff when he got angry.

He then attended Howard University in Washington, D.C., and quickly demonstrated a natural talent for marketing and promotion. Even though he was living and going to school in the nation's capital, he made a fearless and crazy decision to take an unpaid intern job at New York's Uptown Records. He traveled back and forth between the two cities, juggling class work and intern work. When he quickly moved all the way to the top of the corporate ladder at Uptown, he left his school days and Howard University behind. An entrepreneur was about to be born.

The list of music artists he would discover and develop began to grow, starting with Jodeci and Mary J. Blige. But the Uptown job didn't last; he was fired in 1993 and quickly started his own company, Bad Boy Records, taking then-newcomer The Notorious B.I.G. with him. The breakout success of B.I.G.'s *Ready to Die* LP allowed Combs to sign more acts, including Faith Evans, Father MC, and Total, as well as produce records for Usher, Lil' Kim, Mariah Carey, Boyz II Men, Aretha Franklin, and others. Bad Boy had become an East Coast music powerhouse, matched only by its West Coast rival, Death Row Records, led by Tupac Shakur and Suge Knight.

In 1997, Combs moved to the other side of the microphone and recorded his first commercial vocal as a rapper under the name Puff Daddy. His debut single, "Can't Nobody Hold Me Down," spent six weeks at number one on the Billboard Hot 100, and his debut album, *No Way Out*, won the 1998 Grammy for best rap album. A star was born.

With everything going his way, he made another fearless move and started his own clothing line, Sean John, also in 1998.

Success would not come easy, however, and not without controversy—plenty of it. In fact, controversy had saddled Combs even back in his Uptown Records days. In 1991, he had promoted a concert headlined by Heavy D at the City College of New York gymnasium. The event was oversold to twice its capacity, and thousands more without tickets crowded around outside the building the night of the concert. To keep those fans out, Combs's people shut and blocked the only door to a stairwell. When the outsiders broke several glass doors trying to get in, a stampede ensued inside the gym as the concertgoers rushed the blocked stairwell door. Nine people died; Combs, Heavy D, and City College were found liable in a civil suit.

The negative headlines continued into the Bad Boy days, most famously in late 1999 when Combs and then-girlfriend Jennifer Lopez were at Club New York, a trendy midtown Manhattan nightclub. Gunfire broke out, and Combs and fellow rapper Shyne were arrested for weapons violations and other charges. The case got dicier when Combs's driver claimed Combs tried to bribe him to take the gun (and the fall) after the shooting.

Combs was represented by Johnnie Cochran and Benjamin Brafman in the highly publicized trial that followed. He was found not guilty on all charges, but Shyne was convicted and sentenced to 10 years in prison. Later, the driver sued Combs for emotional distress and settled out of court.

It was after all that stress and drama that Combs changed his stage name from Puff Daddy to P. Diddy. But there was even more controversy to come, this time with the clothing line. In 2003, reports surfaced that the Honduran factories producing the Sean John line were paying sweatshop wages and providing far-from-ideal working conditions. Within months, Combs made changes, greatly improving working conditions and even allowing a union. "I'm as pro-worker as they get," he told the press.[16]

Then in 2006, Macy's department store yanked Sean John hooded jackets from its shelves because it had learned the "faux" fur used for the hoods was, in fact, from a real animal, the raccoon dog. Again, Combs moved quickly to minimize the PR damage, stopping use of the fur in the hoodie manufacture and even appearing in a Macy's commercial to smooth things over.

Through the ups and downs, Combs consistently demonstrated an ability to react to the next challenge, fix it, and move on. Slowly, his business acumen and instincts were acknowledged and even admired.

So what did he do during and after all that? He made even more fearless and crazy career decisions: he landed more acting gigs. Building on his acclaimed work in the movies *Made* and *Monster's Ball*, he earned major roles in *Carlito's Way: Rise to Power* and the critically acclaimed Broadway revival of *A Raisin in the Sun*. He broadened his musical

---

16 "P. Diddy in Sweatshop Row," BBC News, October 29, 2003, http://news.bbc.co.uk/2/hi/americas/3222521.stm.

48 producing and collaborations beyond rap, working with David Bowie, Britney Spears, and 'N Sync. In 2002, he made his own reality TV show, *Making the Band 2*. In 2003, he ran the New York Marathon, finishing in a respectable 4 hours, 14 minutes, and 54 seconds. In 2004, he headed the controversial "Vote or Die" campaign for that year's presidential election.

In August 2005, he appeared on the *Today* show and announced he was dropping the "P" in his nom de plume and from now on would simply refer to himself as "Diddy." But even this simple decision was not without controversy, as London-based musical artist Richard "Diddy" Dearlove sought an injunction from the Royal Courts of Justice. Again, there was an out-of-court settlement, and Combs remains P. Diddy—not Diddy—in the United Kingdom.

Then in 2006, he produced his first album in four years, *Press Play*, with guest appearances by a long list of recording stars. The album reached number one in its first week on the charts. He opened an upscale restaurant chain called Justin's (after his son). He launched a cologne brand called I Am King, dedicated to Barack Obama, Muhammad Ali, and Martin Luther King Jr. He promoted his clothing line on huge Times Square billboards. He signed a profit-sharing agreement to develop and promote the Cîroc vodka brand. He acquired clothing line Enyce from Liz Claiborne. He established a business leadership school in New York City. He continues to act in TV series and movies, including two *CSI: Miami* appearances in 2009, a brief role in the 2010 film *Get Him to the Greek*, and a 2011 appearance in the CBS hit *Hawaii Five-0*. He released his latest album, *Last Train to Paris*.[17]

49

Sean Combs's marketing and promotion tactics are at once simple and bold: He knows that he is the brand. He is not shy about promoting that brand anywhere and everywhere. He remains on the cutting edge of technology, using social media and online videos very effectively. He aligns himself with other successful brands. And of course, he reinvents himself again and again. The man and his life are never boring, never stale.

What next? Well, he's Sean Combs, after all, and whatever it is, under whatever name, it will surprise and amaze. Certainly it'll be a lot fearless and just a little crazy. And it will promote the brand—the man himself.

■ ■ ■

➡ MY TAKE

The American Marketing Association (AMA) defines a brand as a "name, term, design, symbol, or any other feature that identifies one seller's good or service as distinct from those of other sellers."[18] Makes sense. That's the traditional marketplace definition of brand; we usually think of something like that when we hear or read the word.

But that definition is just the beginning. A brand can be and should be so much more. A good brand:

---

17 DiddyDirtyMoney.com, http://www.diddydirtymoney.com/default.aspx#!all.

18 "Resource Library: Dictionary," American Marketing Association, http://www.marketingpower.com/_layouts/Dictionary.aspx?dLetter=B.

➨ Delivers the message clearly
➨ Confirms your credibility
➨ Connects with your target prospects emotionally
➨ Motivates the buyer
➨ Solidifies user loyalty[19]

A brand is something you build every day. You nurture it, you grow it, you shout it from the rooftops. Most important, you live it. You must spend time researching, defining, and building your brand. You're thinking about your brand at every step in my life-wealth strategy—from vision, planning, and execution, on through marketing, networking, and being flexible to deal with the unknowns.

Your brand is your promise to your consumer; it's the challenge to your competition and the threat to your enemy. A successful brand is so much more than a trademarked product name. It stands for something beyond the words. Sometimes the person—the entrepreneur, the celebrity, or the historical figure—is the brand.

Your brand resides within the hearts and minds of customers, clients, prospects, family, friends, and enemies. It is the sum total of their experiences and perceptions, some of which you can influence and some of which you cannot.

Let's look at some types and characteristics of brands, as outlined by branding experts Merriam Associates:

---

19 Laura Lake, "What Is Branding and How Important Is It to Your Marketing Strategy?" About.com, http://marketing.about.com/cs/brandmktg/a/whatisbranding.htm.

- Acronyms: names made of initials—UPS or IBM
- Descriptive brands: names that describe a product ben- 51
  efit or function—Whole Foods or Airbus
- Alliterative and rhyming brands: names that are fun to
  say and stick in the mind—Reese's Pieces or Dunkin'
  Donuts
- Evocative brands: names that evoke a vivid image—
  Amazon or Crest
- Neologisms: completely made-up words—Wii or Kodak
- Foreign words: words adopted from another language—
  Volvo or Samsung
- Founders' names: the names of the people who started it
  all—Hewlett-Packard or Disney
- Geographical brands: brands named for regions, coun-
  tries, or landmarks—Canada Dry or Fujifilm
- Personified brands: Names of mythical characters
  (Nike), fictional characters (Betty Crocker), or real
  people (Trump)
- Brandnomers: Brand names that have become a generic
  term for a product or service—Band-Aid or Kleenex or
  Xerox[20]

Keeping all this in mind, let's take another look at our
three brand case studies. First, Virgin is an intriguing brand
name, hinting at something a little racy or suggestive. But the
brand's high-profile, activist celebrity creator has never had a

---

20 Merriam Associates, "Styles and Types of Company and Product Names,"
http://merriamassociates.com/2009/02/styles-and-types-of-company-and-
product-names/.

whiff of scandal, and Virgin has become a powerful business name with a sheen of innocence and integrity.

Second, truTV works beautifully as a brand, describing at a glance what it is ("actuality" television) and even using some alliteration too. Its former name, Court TV, was effective as well. You saw or read the name, and you knew just what you'd be getting.

Third, Diddy is a perfect example of deliberate, planned brand creation, brand management, and brand promotion. Sean Combs (in whatever name) is the master brand, with subbrands beneath the overall umbrella brand. Have there been starts and stops, flops and failures for the Diddy/Sean Combs brand? Certainly. After all, Combs is fearless and crazy. The man and his brand have become all but indistinguishable. He'll be studied in Harvard Business School someday (if he isn't already).

What about you? What do you do to promote yourself and to establish your personal brand? It all begins—and sometimes ends—with the basics. Because what people see is what they think they'll get.

Whether you think of it as charisma or charm, fearlessness or boldness, the way you present yourself to people is going to have a major impact on your success, both in business and in life. In most business situations, of course, you are simply who you appear to be. As that tired old marketing saying goes, "Perception is reality." But just because it's tired and overused doesn't mean it isn't true. In fact, it's a very profound statement—so profound it merits repeating: "Perception *is* reality."

In essence, that statement says that regardless of what the

truth may be, what someone *believes to be true* is more important, more commanding, and more powerful than the truth   53
itself. (We're talking marketing and branding here, not love
and marriage.)

The statement applies to people at all levels of virtually
all businesses. And it's a companion piece to another old
saw—one that's almost its flip side: "Don't judge a book by
its cover."

The truth is that people all around you do just that. And
when you're striving to be successful, it's important that you
get people to judge you the right way, the way you want to
be perceived. Depending on the situation and the observers,
you might want them to see you as a stable voice of reason,
the calm in a storm, a master of the universe. Other times,
you may want them to be a little uneasy about you, not so
sure. You don't want to be predictable or easy to peg. So you
do your fearless and crazy thing—not psychologically unbal-
anced and totally reckless but fearless and crazy with a plan.

In both social and business settings, people will immediately begin to form impressions about you based on how
you appear and how you present yourself. And much of that
evaluation will occur in extremely subtle ways—so subtle, in
fact, that you will probably not even be aware of the "tag" a
person puts on you.

If you're perceived negatively in a social setting, the result
may not mean more than a lost opportunity to meet someone
special. But in a business context, it can mean a lost job offer,
a lost promotion, a lost infusion of investor capital, or a lost
million-dollar deal. And when you are taking the step to be
crazy and fearless in your approach to business, you just can't

afford to lose because of something as changeable, as affected by your direct influence, as appearance and perception.

54

Knowing that perception does count will give you added strength as you travel in business and social circles. This doesn't mean you should adopt a phony persona just to create the desired perception in the mind of the person in front of you at a particular time. It's more important to be yourself, to be genuine and sincere, to be real, than it is to try to sell a fake image—which, sooner or later, will come crashing down around you.

Because you know how important perception can be, you can tailor your behavior so that it's appropriate for the surroundings you're in and for the people you're among. You can avoid putting on false airs and be genuine, sincere, and real, even as you are perfectly attuned to the environment around you—be it a farm field in Iowa or a Tiffany's in Manhattan.

As an example, I was recently in a very nice department store in Beverly Hills, and while looking at men's fashions, I happened to overhear a mother in her late twenties talking to her six- or seven-year-old son, who was becoming more than a little rambunctious.

"No, Darren, please use your 'inside' voice," she said to the boy.

She wasn't telling her son not to be a six- or seven-year-old. She was merely asking him to be conscious of his surroundings and to modify his behavior so that it was appropriate for the sense of decorum and ambience in that store.

Obviously, it wasn't the first time he had heard that request, delivered by her in a very warm, sincere, and loving—but firm—way, and he responded immediately. I could tell that this aware, caring mother was teaching her young son about personal bearing and his responsibility to his surroundings and the other people in the store.

I could also tell his character hadn't been scarred, his soul hadn't been injured, and his six- or seven-year-old self-esteem hadn't been assaulted. He did as he had been asked, without a fight, without disagreement, and without complaint.

I'm sure that young mother has spent quality time teaching her son about the importance of being aware of who he is as a person and how his behavior affects the impression people have of him, and—more important—how his behavior affects the physical and mental well-being of those around him. In other words, if he's a brat, he'll ruin their day.

I'm sure she also has taught him the value of recognizing that a particular type of behavior may be acceptable in one environment but unacceptable in another. The way he acts on a playground is one thing, while the way he acts in a quiet, genteel department store is quite another. And of course, there is his school behavior, his dining room table behavior, his bedroom behavior, his in-the-SUV behavior, and so on.

The truth is that in business, as in life, behavior is situational. Obvious? Of course. But sometimes—and not just with six-year-olds—what's obvious is far from common.

We all need to be conscious of where we are, who is around us, and what our objectives are at any given moment. We should be aware of how our behavior, dress, choice of words, and even thoughts may either complement our surroundings and our "mission" in that environment or clash with them and work against us.

Watching that interaction between the young mother and

her son was confirmation for me that while perception *is* reality, we are continually in situations in which we can shape and influence the perceptions people have. By managing the perception, we create the reality.

That said, it should be noted that it is harder to *change a perception already formed* than it is *to establish an initial perception*. To use the fearless and crazy approach to business and life to your best advantage, you should not only use it at the appropriate times and in the appropriate situations, but you should use it after you have established a positive perception, a solid reputation, and a successful track record. If you're already perceived as unstable, untrustworthy, and unreliable, then suddenly making a move that's fearless and crazy won't have much of an impact. People will shrug their shoulders and walk away.

One of my favorite pieces of image/branding advice is "Carry your briefcase, but wear your portfolio."

At first blush, the line may suggest that you should walk around with a briefcase to send a message to those around you that you are a serious businessperson, a person of depth and substance. It may also seem to suggest that you should always wear expensive, top-of-the-line clothes, thereby sending a second message: *I am so successful that I can afford to spend unnecessary money on business attire when everyday clothes would be just as good!*

But that's not what I'm getting at; that's not what the advice means. The first half of the line—carry your brief-case—merely suggests that, yes, you can present yourself as a serious businessperson with the accessories and typical business tools you take with you, but you don't necessarily need to carry phony props just to make an impression. And please don't ever correct someone who comments about your brief-case by saying, "It's not a briefcase; it's an *attaché* case." Ouch. Think about what kind of perception that creates.

The second half of the line—but wear your portfolio—doesn't mean wear your stock portfolio or artwork portfolio or résumé or vita. What I'm talking about is your *professional bearing*. That's your "portfolio" in this context, and it's far more important than your net-worth statement. It's what will allow you to grow and prosper, to accumulate wealth and income—in short, to be successful.

In fact, I recently had a discussion with a marketing con-sultant about this very point. I was talking about wealth and income, in that order, and he corrected me, saying that "income should come first, and that creates wealth."

Well, to me, wealth is a state of mind. Once you have adopted that state of mind, you can then begin to generate the income you want. It may sound a little new age-y, like all you have to do is have happy thoughts about wealth, and the money will come rolling your way. No, not exactly. In fact, it's much more than that. Don't laugh and dismiss it just yet. It's fearless and crazy, and trust me, it pays off. It's what Chapter 1 was all about—life-wealth. If you live life in a wealthy, successful, confident manner, you *are* wealthy, suc-cessful, and confident. Wealth for life; life for wealth.

Wealth: think it, envision it, build it, earn it. That's what I mean by *wear your portfolio.* Wear your success and achieve-ment—your *wealth*—almost as if it were an article of clothing you could put on. If you do wear it everywhere you go—wear it, not flaunt it—you will quickly realize everything you do as a businessperson, including your behavior, your bearing, your actions and decisions, and even your thoughts, will manifest the new you, will create the perception of success and confidence—the perception of *wealth*. And that perception, that brand, will be your reality.

4

AGAINST TYPE

Do not follow where the path may lead. Go, instead, where there is no path and leave a trail.

—RALPH WALDO EMERSON

Going against the grain, leaving your comfort zone, changing for the sake of change, shaking things up—all these familiar phrases describe fearless and crazy moments when a person or a business does a 180 and makes a decision contrary to what that person or business seems to be about. The only responses are "WTF?!" "How could that happen?!" "He/she/it would never do that! But he/she/it did!"

Applying these fearless and crazy strategies in your business can pay off. Just when they think they know you, just when they think they're comfortable with everything you are

and do, you pitch them a sweeping curveball that knocks
their socks off. And you can reap the rewards; you can do
just what you want to do. They'll never look at you the same
again.

In from the Cold

The headlines had jaws dropping everywhere: NIXON IN
CHINA screamed the large black type on just about every
newspaper in just about every country in the world. Richard
M. Nixon?! Thirty-seventh president of the United States?
The conservative politician who had made his name and his
fame as a Commie-basher, an enemy of all things Red? In
China? Chairman Mao Zedong's China? The secretive, vio-
lent Middle Kingdom of the Cultural Revolution? The Communist cohort of our current battlefield adversary, North
Vietnam? *That* China? *That* Nixon? Had the planet spun off
of its axis?

Well, yes, in a way. It was February 1972, and President
Richard M. Nixon had just made a fearless and crazy decision: he would pay a visit to his country's Cold War enemy,
the People's Republic of China, the very same nation he'd
been railing about since it went Communist in 1949 and the
United States cut all diplomatic ties.

But Nixon didn't just wake up one morning and tell his
staff to roll Air Force One out of the hangar, we're going to
China. His fearless and crazy decision was methodically and
meticulously planned. And—incredibly—in an era of almost
steady leaks from government insiders to the press, Nixon

and his inner circle pulled off the surprise. They made those jaws hit the floor.

It began in 1969, shortly after Nixon moved into the White House. Sure, he was still a staunch anti-Communist, but he was also a realist, especially when it came to foreign affairs. He recognized that the People's Republic of China and the Union of Soviet Socialist Republics (USSR) were more and more in disagreement over just about everything, including their shared, contested border. There was no such thing as a giant Communist monolith ready to take over the world. Instead, there were two major camps, each suspicious of the other. Nixon felt he could successfully play one off of the other, even as we continued our war in Vietnam. The era of détente was at hand.

The president decided to work the diplomatic back channels through Warsaw, Poland, with Henry Kissinger, his national security advisor, as his point man. Walter Stoessel Jr., our ambassador to Poland, made the initial contact with his Chinese counterparts at a fashion show at the Yugoslavian embassy in Warsaw.[21]

Stoessel was a State Department employee, of course, and when his superiors back in Washington got wind of the Nixon/Kissinger-ordered overture, they expressed their concerns to the White House. Nixon responded in typical Nixonian fashion: he got mad and cut them out of the loop, keeping even Secretary of State William Rogers on the

---

21 "Foreign Affairs, February 21-28, 1972," United States History, http://www.u-s-history.com/pages/h1877.html.

outside.[22] Kissinger would handle the intrigue and the secret diplomacy. And he loved it.

Next, Pakistan president Yahya Khan passed along personal greetings from Nixon to Chinese premier Zhou Enlai, the country's most powerful man now that Mao was in his final years. Zhou replied through Khan that he would "consider" Nixon's visit proposal and let him know later.[23]

It was Chairman Mao himself who kept the initiative alive with an April 1971 invitation to the U.S. table tennis team to visit China after its tour in Japan. Thus ping-pong diplomacy was born. Like Nixon, Mao was eager to play power politics. By extending a hand to America, he would make his Soviet adversaries nervous. Plus, he could continue his ongoing push for the return of Taiwan to the People's Republic, where he felt it rightfully belonged.

About six months after the successful table tennis team visit, Mao sent a secret message to Nixon, inviting the U.S. president to visit. But first the United States must quietly send a special envoy to make the arrangements and plan the details. The special envoy? Kissinger, of course.

On July 1, 1971, Kissinger embarked on a routine tour of Asia, with the first stop in Pakistan. President Khan was in on the ruse. The secret plan was code-named Marco Polo. At an embassy dinner, Kissinger feigned illness and temporarily excused himself. He and his small entourage of assistants and bodyguards secretly headed for the airport (though even his entourage wasn't fully apprised of the plan). When they got

---

22 Ibid.

23 Ibid.

on the unmarked airplane, they were greeted by four Chinese soldiers in Mao jackets. Kissinger's guards at first thought they were being kidnapped.[24]

Kissinger flew to China, made the arrangements in less than 48 hours, and returned to Pakistan, now feeling much better and ready to continue his scheduled Asian tour.

More secret messages followed, ironing out more details. Both sides knew that the symbolism of the visit was more important than any substantive agreements. Those, hopefully, could come in due time. Later Nixon wrote, "We were embarking on a voyage of philosophical discovery as uncertain, and in some ways as perilous, as the voyages of geographical discovery of an earlier time."[25]

Nixon landed in Beijing on February 17, 1972. He met with Chairman Mao, a moment televised around the world. But Nixon's most important sessions were with Zhou Enlai. Vietnam (China wanted the United States out) and Taiwan (China wanted it back) were the two major contentious issues, and neither side was expecting resolution. The final agreement—the Shanghai Communiqué—signed at the end of the visit was in many ways a typical diplomatic document with language vague enough to allow each side to smile and both to declare progress.

At the final banquet, a triumphant and slightly tipsy Nixon raised his glass in salute: "This has been the week that changed the world!"[26]

---

24 Ibid.

25 Ibid.

26 Ibid.

Indeed it had. After Nixon's fearless and crazy decision, nothing would be the same again. China was brought onto the world stage, and the USSR was forced to rethink its own geopolitical strategy. In fact, within a few weeks, Nixon was in Moscow negotiating the beginning of the Strategic Arms Limitation Talks (SALT). From then on, the world superpowers would look to discussion, diplomacy, and accommodation when dealing with each other. The decades-long tensions of the Cold War were easing.

As for Nixon himself, the rest of his story is familiar. But despite the Watergate debacle and the resignation and fall from grace, not even Nixon's fiercest enemies could ever deny his expertise in foreign affairs. He was savvy enough to sense the opening, and he made it happen. He knew that who he was and what he stood for made the initiative that much more dramatic, that much more significant.

Fearless and crazy, yes. And the world is better for it.

Charity Write-off

It wasn't that long ago that being a millionaire was a big deal. There was a black-and-white TV series called *The Millionaire*, and Marilyn Monroe, Betty Grable, and Lauren Bacall starred in a 1953 movie, *How to Marry a Millionaire*, showing women how to do just that. No question about it: back then, having a million dollars meant you were rich.

Well, millionaires are no big deal anymore, especially when you count assets and investments. Millionaires are sprinkled throughout society. You may be one yourself. I am.

It's the *billionaires* who get our attention these days. And
the man at the top of the billionaire list, the richest man   65
in the world at $74 billion and counting, is an unassuming
Mexican citizen of Lebanese descent named Carlos Slim.
He's so unassuming that, despite his wealth and fame, he still
drives his own car to work every day—in a country notorious
for violence and kidnappings.[27]

His business empire is vast. In fact, some sources say it's
impossible to go through a day in Mexico without interacting with a Carlos Slim enterprise. That's primarily because
of telecommunications, the foundation of his wealth. He is
chairman and CEO of Telmex and América Móvil and has
extensive holdings in other Mexican companies through his
conglomerate Grupo Carso SAB. And of course, he has various holdings throughout the world.

Telmex is the big one, however. It's Mexico's dominant
telephone company, controlling 90 percent of the country's
landlines. So yes, it's difficult not to interact with a Carlos
Slim company in the course of a day. Slim and his family own
49.1 percent of Telmex.

Slim takes some heat for being so rich in a country that
is anything but. The per capita income in Mexico is about
$14,500 a year, with almost 17 percent of the population
living in poverty. Slim's incredible wealth is about 5 percent
of Mexico's annual economic output. But Slim doesn't give
much heed to the critics. "When you live for others' opinions,

---

27 Harriet Alexander, "Carlos Slim: At Home with the World's Richest Man,"
The Telegraph, February 19, 2011, http://www.telegraph.co.uk/finance/8335604/
Carlos-Slim-At-home-with-the-worlds-richest-man.html.

you are dead," he says. "I don't want to live thinking about how I'll be remembered."[28]

It's this approach to his legacy that has recently set Carlos Slim on a different path from his fellow famous billionaires. Slim, in his calm and considered way, is going fearlessly against type and taking a unique stance.

Bill Gates (the world's second-richest person) and Warren Buffett (the third) have received much acclaim—deservedly so—for their campaign to get the super rich of the world to pledge at least half of their accumulated fortunes to charity upon their deaths. They call it the Giving Pledge. Gates and Buffett have spread their message of goodwill and good deeds throughout the world, even to China. Hundreds of the über-wealthy have signed the pledge, and more do so every day. It's the kind of noble effort and do-the-right-thing campaign that elicits smiles and nods and makes us all feel there may yet be hope for the planet. Nobody could be against the billionaires' pledge.

Nobody except Carlos Slim. He thinks it's well-meaning but wrongheaded. "What we need to do as businessmen is to help to solve the problems, the social problems," he explains. "To fight poverty, but not by charity." Corporations and businesses do that best, says Slim, when they run successful, expanding companies that provide jobs for thousands, improve infrastructure, develop new facilities, and generate dynamic markets. The billionaires' money needs to be

---

28 Helen Coster, "Carlos Slim Helu Now World's Second-Richest Man," forbes. com, April 11, 2007, http://www.forbes.com/2007/04/11/billionaires-helu-telecom-biz-cz_hc_0411helu.html.

reinvested in the various enterprises and societies from which it was generated in the first place. Don't wait for death; do it now. Put more back in, and even more will come back out. And so many more people will benefit. Besides, donating the pledged money to charity will result in huge tax deductions, depriving governments of much-needed tax revenue.[29]

Slim is clearly marching to a different drummer than Gates, Buffett, and the others who've signed the pledge. But is he just being a tightwad? Is he hoarding his wealth so he can be number one forever? Hardly.

In fact, Carlos Slim does give; he does provide for others. But he does it his way, demanding realistic, measurable results. He doesn't hand out big checks. He finances boots-on-the-ground programs and initiatives, similar, ironically, to the work of the Bill & Melinda Gates Foundation.

The focus of his Carlos Slim Foundation is education and health care. Current projects include a $100 million medical initiative to perform 50,000 cataract surgeries in Peru, the creation of a $20 million fund to strengthen small and medium-size businesses in Colombia, and a digital education program for youth in Mexico. His foundation is also spending $150 million on programs in nutrition and disease prevention in Central America. He has donated $50 million to work with the World Wildlife Fund to restore six areas for endangered species in Mexico, including the monarch butterfly. The Carlos Slim Foundation has also pledged $100

---

29 Keerthikasingaravel, "Carlos Slim and the Giving Pledge," *Wealthymatters,* August 1, 2011, http://wealthymatters.com/2011/08/01/carlos-slim-and-the-giving-pledge/.

million to Colombian singer Shakira's ALAS Foundation, which creates education programs for young people.[30]

Slim believes in charitable giving that creates productive, working citizens. And so he targets cataract operations that will allow the recipients to return to gainful employment and digital education programs that will create a generation of computer-savvy Mexican youth.

Maybe Carlos Slim's ideas about charity aren't really so crazy and different after all. They sound a lot like that oft-quoted Chinese proverb: "Give a man a fish and you feed him for a day; teach a man to fish and you feed him for a lifetime."

Don't expect Carlos Slim to give you a fish.

A Woman's Place

She certainly didn't realize it at the time, but in 1832, at the age of 11, Clara Barton had found her life's calling. Her older brother, David, fell from the rafters of the family's unfinished barn and injured himself severely. Young Clara attended to him for three years, eventually nursing him back to health. She even administered his "great, crawling, loathsome leeches," as she called them, a standard treatment at the time.[31]

---

30 "Slim's Big Giveaway," March 5, 2007, *Bloomberg Businessweek*, March 5, 2007, http://www.businessweek.com/magazine/content/07_10/b4024065.htm? campaign_id=rss_magzn.

31 Percy Harold Epler, *The Life of Clara Barton* (New York: The Macmillan Company, 1915), 12, http://books.google.com/books?id=LC5x31cCf_sC&pg= PA12 &source=gbs_toc_r&cad=4#v=onepage&q&f=false.

As she began an adult life of her own, she became first a teacher, when few in that profession were female. She then found employment with the government, again when few bureaucratic posts were held by women.

She was working as a clerk in the U.S. Patent Office in Washington, D.C., in April 1861, when the Civil War began. On April 19, a week after the firing on Fort Sumter had started it all, troops from the Sixth Massachusetts arrived in Washington in disarray, having been attacked by secessionists in Baltimore. Barton herself was born and raised in Massachusetts, and she knew many of these men and their families. She and her sister, Sally, went to the station to meet the soldiers but were dismayed to learn that the city had nowhere to billet the troops or care for the wounded among them. Many were housed in the Capitol building itself. Barton took the most seriously wounded to her sister's house and nursed them; she collected donated food and supplies from local merchants. The frantic work inspired her. "The patriot blood of my fathers was warm in my veins," she wrote later.

More troops soon arrived in the chaotic city, this time from upstate New York and New Jersey. She visited the men camped in and around the city. "I don't know how long it has been since my ear has been free from the roll of a drum," she wrote her father. "It is the music I sleep by, and I love it."[32]

Again, and from then on, there was the need for supplies—everything from blankets to bandages. Barton became the recipient of supplies sent to Washington in response to

---

32 Joan Goodwin, "Clara Barton," Unitarian Universalist Association, http://www25.uua.org/uuhs/duub/articles/clarabarton.html.

letters the men wrote home. When floods of the wounded filled the city after the first battle of Manassas (Bull Run), she began soliciting supplies from various civic groups and relief committees. "I will remain here while anyone remains," she wrote. "I may be compelled to face danger, but never fear it, and while our soldiers can stand and fight, I can stand and feed and nurse them."[33]

All that good and necessary work would have been plenty for most women or men, but Clara Barton had a fearless and crazy desire to do even more, to work where her nursing and organizational skills were most needed and could be most effective: at the battlefield.

She pleaded and petitioned every decision maker she could find, from politicians to military officers. She wanted to be out there where the bullets were flying and the blood was flowing. She would even bring her own medical supplies. She was turned down again and again. We appreciate your nursing and your supplies, of course, they said. Continue to roll bandages; continue to contact families. Our nation is grateful. But don't go where you don't belong. War is a man's horror show. It is no place for a lady.

Finally in August 1862, she somehow obtained a quarter-master's pass and six wagons with teamsters to carry her supplies to the front lines. A few days after the battle of Cedar Mountain in northern Virginia, she appeared at a field hospital at midnight with a wagonload of supplies drawn by a four-mule team. The surgeon on duty, overwhelmed by the human disaster surrounding him, wrote later, "I thought that

---

33 Ibid.

night if heaven ever sent out an angel, she must be one—her
assistance was so timely."[34]

She and her two helpers worked among the Cedar Mountain wounded for two days and nights without food or sleep,
even tending to wounded Confederate prisoners.

From then on she was known as "The Angel of the Battlefield." Clara Barton nursed the troops at the battles of
Fairfax Station, Chantilly, Harpers Ferry, South Mountain,
Antietam, Fredericksburg, Charleston, Petersburg, and Cold
Harbor. She never hung back with the medical units, waiting
for the wounded to be brought to her. Instead, she pressed
forward, fearless and a little crazy, to the scene of the carnage.

At Antietam, she ordered the drivers of her supply wagons
to follow the cannon and traveled all night, pulling ahead
of military medical units. While the battle raged, she and
her associates dashed about bringing relief and hope to the
field. She nursed, comforted, and cooked for the wounded.
She later wrote that in the face of danger, "I always tried
. . . to succor the wounded until medical aid and supplies
could come up. I could run the risk; it made no difference to
anyone if I were shot or taken prisoner."[35]

In April 1865, four years after the war had begun, it ended.
Surrender. Peace.

But for Barton, the war left much still to be done. First
on that long list was to account for the missing. She had
already begun that task during the fighting by writing letters,

---

34 "Clara Barton: Founder of the American Red Cross," American Red Cross,
redcross.org, http://www.redcross.org/museum/history/claraBarton.asp.

35 Ibid.

asking questions, and keeping records. A few weeks before
his assassination, President Abraham Lincoln acknowledged
her work on behalf of the missing and their families. Lincoln
wrote, "To the Friends of Missing Persons: Miss Clara Barton
has kindly offered to search for the missing prisoners of war.
Please address her . . . giving her the name, regiment, and
company of any missing prisoner."[36]

Barton established the Office of Correspondence with
Friends of the Missing Men of the United States Army and
operated it out of her rooms in Washington for the next four
years. She and her assistants received and answered more
than 63,000 letters and identified more than 22,000 missing
men.[37]

She didn't know it then, but her tireless labor during and
after the war was foreshadowing what would later be her
most lasting legacy: the American Red Cross. She founded
the organization, modeled on the International Red Cross,
in May 1881 and became its first president.

But perhaps none of this would have occurred, and certainly not for Clara Barton, had she not fearlessly insisted
on moving toward the heat of battle, not away from it. As
she wrote later, "The door that nobody else will go in seems
always to open widely for me."[38]

---

36 Ibid.

37 Ibid.

38 Ishbel Ross, *Angel of the Battlefield* (New York: Harper & Brothers, 1956),
http://quotes.dictionary.com/the_door_that_nobody_else_will_go.

■ ■ ■

➡ MY TAKE

Going against type is a little bit like using the element of surprise (discussed in Chapter 2). They can both mean fearless and crazy moments that put people back on their heels and give that fearless and crazy person a decided advantage. But there's a major difference between the two. As described in Chapter 2, General Douglas MacArthur executed a startling strategic maneuver in warfare; Groupon surprises us with its unexpected business decisions; and Muhammad Ali pulled off a terrific tactical surprise during his battle in the ring. But these three were not going against type. MacArthur was a general, Groupon is an online business enterprise, and Ali was a boxer. They were and are practicing their professions, doing what they always do, and staying true to their calling—finding and fighting a way to victory.

But as discussed in this chapter, Nixon, Slim, and Barton all went against what they and others like them had always stood for. The Cold Warrior hobnobbing with Commies. The unassuming billionaire rejecting the praiseworthy initiative of his fellow billionaires. The genteel woman showing up at the front line.

All three were being contrarian, going against the grain, against the conventional wisdom. They were questioned about it and criticized for it, but they stood their ground. And the world is a better, more interesting place because they did.

Even though I'm still a young man, I have frequently gone against type, against the grain, in my professional and

74

business life. For example, I decided early on to carry a minimum of debt, using cash instead of credit cards whenever possible. Conventional wisdom for business says you should use someone else's money, not your own, whenever possible. Conventional wisdom says that leverage and credit are good things. When used properly and prudently, leverage and credit can allow you to start and expand a business. They can help you make that next big leap; they can be the difference between success and failure. That's what banks, investors, bonds—just about every financial facet of capitalism—are all about. Borrow money today so you can flourish; then pay it back tomorrow.

A credit card, of course, is leverage at its most basic. We frequently hear stories of folks using their credit cards to jump-start their restaurant, finance their movie, or lease that first office. And as you'll recall from this book's introduction, that's exactly how I got started in the 1990s—using credit card debt. It was one of my first fearless and crazy decisions.

But I have since contradicted my own history and success and come out against type, against the conventional wisdom for leverage and borrowing. I'm against credit cards. You'll read more about my thinking on this in Chapter 10.

My most significant against-the-grain decision came after I had completed my financial industry training and internship and was ready to step out into the big, bad world. Friends and family members assumed I would get a salaried position with a reputable investment firm and gradually work my way up the corporate ladder. I would earn my salary and commissions, build seniority at the firm, and settle into a slow, satisfying career. That's what having a career means, everyone said.

But I had a different plan, one I'd researched for hours in libraries and bookstores and in meetings with respected professionals. Even though I was an untested, wet-behind-the-ears rookie, I decided to go to work as an *independent contractor* financial advisor for a small boutique financial services firm called The Griffin Agency. No traditional career path for me. "Arthur, are you crazy?" asked my friends from college.

Yes, I guess I was. Fearless and crazy. And though I didn't realize it at the time, I was setting the foundation for my own life-wealth plan.

At first it looked like those college friends were right. I seemed to be in free fall to failure. In my first five months as an independent advisor, I didn't make more than $500. My friends, on the other hand, were in the early stages of their traditional career paths and considering new SUVs and new homes in the suburbs. They seemed to have figured things out and would live the American Dream.

Rather than be envious of them and doubt my own plan, I saw the beginnings of their success as an opportunity for me. I would create investment opportunities for them and their friends and relatives. I would help them attain their financial goals and thereby attain my own along the way. I would be their financial advisor.

My plan was simple and powerful, and you'll hear about it frequently in these pages: short-term, mid-term, and long-term goal planning. I developed specific, customized strategies for my friends and clients that would make their great dreams come true by building wealth and protecting their assets. For example, short-term savings strategies could help them buy that new car; mid-term plans could get them that gated-community house; and long-term savings/investment strategies (IRA, 401(k)) could ensure a comfortable, secure retirement not dependent on Social Security (which is far from a sure thing for my generation). I combined these wealth accumulation plans with a solid, systematic debt elimination strategy, including minimizing the use of credit, as mentioned above.

And you know what? It worked. My clients liked what I did and the results I brought in. Word spread. I got referrals and recommendations. I decided to take my independent status one fearless and crazy step further: I started my own company, Arthur Wylie Financial Services. I was going against the grain in a big way, even though I was still in my mid-twenties.

From then on, things happened fast. I moved into a large facility, hired personnel, and began a brand-marketing campaign that quickly got the attention of Charlotte's wealth management profession. Charlotte was second only to New York as the country's premier financial industry city. Being a success there meant something. Consequently, business boomed; we could barely keep up with it.

With so much success, I decided to get my real estate license, start a real estate company to better serve my clients' property investment needs, and of course, keep a greater share of the profits for Arthur Wylie Financial Services. Later I hired a team of real estate brokers to run the operation and expand it into several southeastern states.

We brought in attorneys and accountants to do even more in-depth financial planning and offer more professional services. To the client, it was added value; we were becoming almost a one-stop shop. Clients are the key, of course, and we continually found ways to let them know how much we appreciated them. We had more than 1,200 clients across the country and had facilitated more than $400 million in financial transactions, brokered deals, and managed assets. You name it, we did it.

And Arthur Wylie, this against-type go-getter from North Carolina, was named Young Alumnus of the Year at UNC–Charlotte, featured in numerous national and local publications and broadcasts, and listed in the *Charlotte Business Journal's* top "40 Under 40" in Charlotte. Not bad for starting with zero dollars. I had a small but thought-out plan that allowed me to grow efficiently. I went from college student to entrepreneur. I was working and living my life-wealth plan, even though that's not what I called it back then. My wealth management company and its ancillary businesses brought success and wealth to me and the people who worked for me and, most important, to our many clients.

Incidentally, some of those friends who told me I was crazy for not setting out on the traditional path and working my way up some corporate ladder ended up abandoning that path themselves and working for me—the fearless and crazy guy.

It all happened because I went against type. And that's my simple advice to you: zig when everyone tells you to zag.

5

THE RIGHT THING

It is curious that physical courage should be so common in the world and moral courage so rare.

—MARK TWAIN

Call it what you will—morality, ethics, religious values, the Golden Rule—but in business and in life, doing the right thing trumps all. There is a greater good, something far beyond price-earnings ratios, return on investment, and profit-and-loss statements. In our daily striving to be successful, to make money and grow, we sometimes forget that it is the human balance sheet that is most important. Even if you don't believe in a God of justice and a final reckoning, in your heart of hearts you know that what matters is how you treat the least of those among us.

And just to be realistic, doing that right thing—a fearless and crazy right thing—almost always results in a better business and a better life. What goes around does come around. Do right; you'll feel right. And you just might do well.

Per Diem

A Cleveland newspaper best summarized the effect of the amazing announcement: "It shot like a blinding rocket through the dark clouds of the present industrial depression."[39]

The rocketeer: Henry Ford.

The date: January 5, 1914.

The rocket: In one week from that day, Ford Motor Company workers would from then on be paid an astonishing $5.00 per day, minimum. Henry Ford had just raised his minimum wage from $2.34 a day to the unheard of $5.00. (That's more than $110.00 in current dollar terms.) In addition, the workday would be eight hours and the workweek six days (later reduced to five).

Was the old man out of his mind? Crazy? Why pay all that when you don't have to? Why spoil your workforce? Why eat into your profit margin? Was he trying to be popular? Trying to please the cynics on the outside looking in at his booming automobile business? Hardly. Yes, it was a crazy move. Crazy like a fox—and good for Henry Ford, Ford Motor Company, and, most of all, its thousands of workers.

By late 1913, Henry Ford had problems. His introduction

---

39 *Cleveland Plain Dealer*, January 11, 1914.

of the automated assembly line that year had enabled him to turn out a Model T every 24 seconds, but the overall pro- ductivity per worker wasn't much better than it was in the first year the cars were made. The men hated the repetitive assembly-line work. Absenteeism had reached 10 percent a day, and turnover had climbed to 370 percent. Because of the turnover rate, many Ford departments would hire 300 workers to fill 100 positions just to be sure that every slot would always be filled and the Model T's would roll off the line nonstop.

Ford had invented the ultimate in organizational efficiency. Everything was designed beautifully and working well—everything except his human employees.

So Ford came up with his plan to increase wages and convinced his directors. The company's announcement that January reflected the importance of the decision: "The Ford Motor Company, the greatest and most successful automobile manufacturing company in the world, will, on January 12, inaugurate the greatest revolution in the matter of rewards for its workers ever known in the industrial world."[40]

Later, Ford met with reporters and explained his thinking: "We believe in making 20,000 men prosperous and contented rather than follow the plan of making a few slave drivers in our establishment millionaires."[41]

---

40 "The Revolution of 1914," *Dearborn News Online*, January 5, 2009, http://www.dearbornnewsonline.com/2009/01/revolution-of-1914.html.

41 Samuel Crowther, "Henry Ford: Why I Favor Five Days' Work with Six Days' Pay," *World's Work*, October 1926, http://www.worklessparty.org/timework/ford.htm.

But there was a little more to it than that. Henry Ford was a believer in "welfare capitalism"—a sort of industrial paternalism that said it was important ethically and economically for a corporate employer to provide for its employees' basic human needs. If their lives were satisfying, they would be loyal, productive workers. As we might say today, it would be a win-win.

Ford liked to call his $5.00 per day "profit sharing." And in fact, you didn't just walk in off the street at Ford and start getting the $5.00 your first day. You had to be in the company's employ for six months before the $5.00 kicked in. Also, you had to be at least 22 years of age and live in Detroit. Moreover—and not surprisingly for the times—the plan did not include or even mention women. Ford Motor Company's female workers, who had been earning on average $2.04 per day, did not qualify at all. "I consider women only a temporary factor in industry," Ford explained. "I pay our women well so they can dress attractively and get married."[42]

The new wages and hours would keep the unionism movement at bay for the time being. Who needed a union when you were treated this well? Most important, the handsome pay scale also meant that Ford workers would be able to afford the very vehicles they were producing. The company and the economy would benefit, and both did almost immediately. From 1914 to 1916, Ford Motor Company profits jumped from $30 million to $60 million.

Ford's auto industry competitors throughout Michigan .

---

42 Ray Batchelor, *Henry Ford, Mass Production, Modernism, and Design* (Manchester, UK: Manchester University Press, 1994), 50.

were forced to raise their wages as well or see a drain of talent
away from them and to Ford Motor Company.

Yet there was even more to Ford's version of welfare capitalism. He took it all a bit too far. Besides the six-month
requirement, Ford Motor Company insisted that its
employees conduct their lives in a manner of which Ford's
Sociological Department approved. That meant no heavy
drinking, no gambling, and no abandoning their wives and
children. To be eligible to receive the company's wages and
hours largesse, an employee "must show himself to be sober,
saving, steady, industrious and must satisfy the staff that his
money would not be wasted in riotous living."[43]

The Sociological Department staff utilized 50 investigators
and scores of support personnel to look into possible trans-
gressions, shortcomings, and incidents. Despite the paternal-
istic spying and heavy-handed oversight, the vast majority of
Ford workers qualified and remained qualified for the wages
and working conditions of Ford's profit sharing. And they
most certainly would have done so even without the Sociological Department keeping tabs on them.

Ford's welfare capitalism was highly controversial and thoroughly castigated in the press. Private lives should be—and
are—just that: private. Ford gradually backed off. By the time
he wrote his 1922 memoir, he had abandoned the whole idea
of a Sociological Department and its morality police. "Paternalism has no place in industry," he wrote. "Welfare work
that consists in prying into employees' private concerns is out

---

43 Boris Sanchez de Lozada, "Henry Ford and the Five Dollar Day," Bryant.edu,
http://web.bryant.edu/~ehu/h364proj/summ_99/armoush/page3.html.

of date. Men need counsel and men need help, oftentimes special help; and all this ought to be rendered for decency's sake. But the broad workable plan of investment and participation will do more to solidify industry and strengthen organization than will any social work on the outside."[44]

In other words, when they're at the plant, pay them well and listen to their ideas, and when they go home, let them be.

Henry Ford's fearless and crazy $5.00 per day revolutionized industry, acknowledging the importance of worker morale and respect for worker talents and lives. Most of all, of course, it was just plain smart. Said Ford, "The payment of five dollars a day for an eight-hour day was one of the finest cost-cutting moves we ever made."[45]

Truth or Consequences

Sometimes a fearless and crazy decision is simple—as simple as just walking away. Two hundred years ago, Isabella Baumfree had plenty to walk away from.

Isabella was one of ten or twelve children (the exact number is unknown) of James and Elizabeth Baumfree, both African slaves brought to the New World and sold to the Hardenbergh family of upstate New York. In 1806, nine-year-old Belle, as Isabella was known, was sold at auction along with a flock of sheep for $100 to John Neely of Kingston, New

---

44 Henry Ford, *My Life and Work* (Stilwell, KS: Digireads.com, 2006), 66.

45 Ibid., 74.

York. Neely was a cruel master and was soon beating and raping Belle almost daily.

Neely sold her in 1808 for $105 to Martinus Schryver, a tavern keeper.

Eighteen months later, Schryver sold her for $175 to John Dumont.

In 1815, while still the property of the Dumonts, Belle, now a young woman, fell in love with a slave named Robert from a neighboring farm. But Robert's owner forbade the relationship because any offspring that might result would not be his possessions. So he savagely beat Robert. Belle, who was in fact pregnant with their child, never saw Robert again but later learned he had died of his injuries from the beating.

In 1817, her master, John Dumont, forced her to marry an older slave named Thomas. She had four children with Thomas, one of whom died shortly after birth.

The state of New York had legislated the abolition of slavery, to be effective in July 1827. Dumont had promised Belle her freedom a year before the official emancipation if she would continue to work for him faithfully and productively. But when the time came in 1826, Dumont changed his mind, claiming Belle's recent hand injury made her less productive. She was furious and continued to work just as hard and efficiently to prove Dumont's statement a lie.

Late that year, Belle escaped to freedom, taking her infant daughter with her. She left her other children behind because they would not be legally freed by the state's emancipation order until they had served as bound servants into their twenties. Her escape was not dramatic—no daring scheme, no shotguns fired, no hounds in pursuit. She simply walked away with her baby on her back. As she said later, "I did not run off, for I thought that wicked, but I walked off, believing that to be all right." [46]

She found refuge in the home of Isaac and Maria Van Wagener, who bought her services for $20 from Dumont, covering the remaining months until the state's law would finally set her legally free.

After she became a free person, she sought her son Peter, then five, who had been illegally sold by Dumont to an abusive slave owner in Alabama. She took the issue to court, prevailed, and got her son back. She was the first black woman ever to go to court against a white man and win.

During her stay with the Van Wageners, she had converted to Christianity, and in 1829, she and Peter moved to New York City, where she worked as a housekeeper, first for Elijah Pierson, a Christian evangelist, and later for Robert Matthews, also known as Prophet Matthias.

In 1839, her son Peter shipped out with a whaling ship from Nantucket. She received letters from Peter while he was at sea, but when the ship returned to port in 1842, Peter was not on board, and she never heard from him again.

She was in her mid-forties now and could have lived out her life as a hardworking housekeeper in New York City. But once again she made a life-altering decision, a fearless and crazy choice. And again, like merely walking away, it was simple on the surface: she changed her name. On June 1,

---

46 "Sojourner Truth (Isabella Baumfree)," Women in History, http://www. lkwdpl.org/wihohio/trut-soj.htm.

1843, Isabella Baumfree became Sojourner Truth, because, she told her friends, "The Spirit calls me, and I must go."[47]   87
And go she did—right into the pages of history.

She became a Methodist and traveled the byways and back roads, advocating and preaching for the abolition of slavery. She met and worked with the foremost abolitionists of the time, including William Lloyd Garrison, Frederick Douglass, and David Ruggles.

In 1850, she published her memoir, *Narrative of Sojourner Truth, a Northern Slave*. She purchased a home, and she spoke at the first National Women's Rights Convention.

The next year in Akron, Ohio, she delivered an impromptu speech on racial and gender inequities to the Ohio Women's Convention. Her talk was so stirring and so well received that it later became known as her "Ain't I a Woman?" speech.

She continued to travel and speak about slavery, abolition, and race. She was on a mission. She moved to Harmonia, Michigan, and bought a house and finally gathered some of her family to her side, including a daughter and two grandchildren.

During the Civil War, she helped recruit black troops for the Union cause. One of her grandsons joined. In October 1864, she met President Lincoln.

After the war, she continued her traveling and speaking, including trips back to New York and along the East Coast. She broadened the subject matter of her talks to include prison reform. She spoke vehemently against capital punishment. For several years she worked to get land grants from the

---

47 Ibid.

federal government for former slaves but was unsuccessful. She even met with President Grant to present her argument.

88

Eventually she returned to Michigan, weary from so much travel and so many talks. She died November 26, 1883, at her Battle Creek home. Forty years after being called by the Spirit and taking up the cause, she was finally silent. And at peace.

Sweating the Small Stuff

History is replete with examples of men and women doing the right thing at the right time. Their selfless actions often change the course of human events and make the world a better place to live. You've just read about two of them— Henry Ford, who paid a top wage, and Sojourner Truth, who stood tall against slavery. Few of us in our mostly ordinary lives have the opportunity to make that crucial decision, to alter the flow of history. After all, we're just getting by, day by day.

But there are opportunities in everyone's daily life to make the right decision and do good things. These are small choices, ordinary opportunities that still can resonate and are still important—if not to everyone everywhere, at least to a few. Just ask Dave Steward, founder and chairman of World Wide Technology (WWT), a $3.3 billion private corporation providing technology products, services, and supply chain solutions to companies around the globe.

Steward's journey has been impressive. Born in Chicago in 1951, he grew up in rural Clinton, Missouri. He attended all-black Lincoln School before transferring along with another African American classmate and integrating the previously all-white Franklin School. He earned his high school diploma from Clinton Senior High and a bachelor's degree in business administration from Central Missouri University in 1974. He then went to work.

Everything changed forever for Steward and his family in 1990, when he founded World Wide Technology. Back then he had a staff of four, including friend and partner Jim Kavanaugh, and a mere 4,000 square feet of office space. Today WWT has more than 900 employees and over a million square feet of office and warehouse space. The company is a top supplier for tech giant Cisco and other industry leaders including Dell, IBM, HP, Oracle, and Microsoft. The company is also a leading federal government technology contractor. WWT is the most successful African American–owned business in America.

And a good part of that success is because Steward, WWT chairman, and Kavanaugh, WWT CEO, know little things mean a lot. They know that employees and customers alike will judge them not so much by the business awards they earn or the financial results they tout but by how well they do the small stuff. That's where the rubber meets the road.

For example, in 1993, World Wide Technology was anything but worldwide. In fact, it was struggling to stay afloat, and several employees had jumped ship. During a meeting in the company conference room, Steward and everyone else in the room could see out into the parking lot as a tow truck pulled up to Steward's vehicle and started to hook it up. The boss's car was being repossessed. Steward was mortified.

Instead of making up some tale or expressing false outrage, he calmly told the group that his briefcase was in his car and he needed to go retrieve it. He did so and returned to the meeting, and the tow truck hauled away the car. "Although I was humiliated," said Steward in an interview for *Heart and Soul*, a book by Robert L. Shook that includes a chapter about WWT, "knowing that how I reacted would affect company morale, I didn't dare show my emotions."[48]

He remained calm, and he stuck to business—the meeting at hand. The next morning he drove up in his wife's car and used it for work until things got better and he could get his own vehicle once more. Said a WWT employee who was at the meeting and witnessed the repo, "Dave handled it so nonchalantly, I just thought, 'Well, sometimes you get knocked down, so you just get back on the bike and keep riding.'"[49]

Small stuff. Done right.

As another example—also from those early, uncertain days—WWT had landed a $4 million contract for PCs for the Army Corps of Engineers. The computers would have to be delivered from WWT's base in St. Louis to Omaha, about 350 miles away. It was the company's first big government contract, so the two bosses, Steward and Kavanaugh, decided they'd make the delivery themselves.

They rented a large truck to carry the PC cargo, drove to Omaha, and shared a cheap motel room for the night, where they took turns guarding the truck parked outside

48 Robert L. Shook, *Heart and Soul: Five American Companies That Are Making the World a Better Place* (Dallas, TX: BenBella Books, 2010), 245.

49 Ibid.

their room. The next day, dressed in jeans and sweatshirts, they drove up to the Army Corps of Engineers loading dock and proceeded to unload the computers. Warehouse workers watched, amazed. First of all, drivers rarely if ever unload their own cargo. But then these two guys got back into the cab of their truck and changed into business suits and ties. They drove off to a meeting with Army brass, dropping off their rental truck on the way and renting a car.

At the meeting, one of the officers asked, "Are you the two guys who unloaded the PCs and changed into business suits?"

"Yes, that was us," said Jim. The officer explained that the warehouse workers had called and told the officers what they'd seen. Jim responded, "We wanted to make sure the PCs were there and everything worked out."

Said Dave Steward later, "From that day on, the Army Corps of Engineers has been one of our best advocates, and they still tell that story about the two guys who drove the truck and changed clothes afterward. That's what we did. Whatever it took, we'd do it."[50]

Small stuff. Done right.

In yet another example, on the evening of September 11, 2001, the U.S. Navy needed 400 laptops and servers shipped immediately from WWT to the still-smoldering Pentagon. It was a national security emergency—but all air travel was suspended. The computers and equipment would have to be assembled, packaged, loaded onto trucks, and sent east. Virtually every WWT employee—from administrative assistants

---

50 Ibid., 249.

to sales reps to maintenance staff to top corporate execs—answered the call and showed up that evening to get the job done. They pulled an all-nighter and got the computers out the door the next morning. Later, the U.S. Navy awarded World Wide Technology its coveted Small Business Award.[51]

Small stuff. Done right.

That do-the-right-thing-no-matter-how-fearless-or-crazy attitude flows right from the top, from founder and chairman Dave Steward. He's a devout Christian and bases much of what he does on Jesus and the Bible. Yet he is respectful of the beliefs or lack of belief of anyone in his employ or any one of his clients. "You can apply the Golden Rule to every business as well as all walks of life," he says. "You can also use what Jesus teaches us in Mark 12:31: 'You shall love your neighbor as yourself.' Both of these verses are simple, easy to remember, and can serve as guiding principles on how to conduct business every day for as long as you are in business."[52]

Amen.

■ ■ ■

➡ MY TAKE

The most compelling reason to do the right thing in your personal life is just that: it's right. You know it, others know it, and—if you're a believer—God knows it. When you do the right thing, you walk with the angels. You feel fulfilled, you feel confident, and you are grateful for the opportunity

---

51 Ibid., 254.

52 Ibid., 281.

to have that choice. And the world is grateful that you made it—if not immediately, then later, when the stories are told and the history is written.

When you do the right thing in your business life, you get all that and more. You also have an opportunity to use that decision to solidify your company's stellar reputation and—dare we say it—increase its bottom line. Yes, I realize that sounds crass, manipulative, and conniving. But it's true: do good, and you'll do well. Clients, consumers, partners, and investors all want to deal with and be associated with a company that does right and is consistently ethical—a company that has a corporate conscience, shares its success, and knows that the business doesn't exist in some kind of financial vacuum. It's in the world; it's of the world. And as such, it has responsibilities.

When a company and its CEO (that's you) possess and demonstrate a corporate conscience, they become true symbols of life-wealth—they practice what they preach, and they not only seem all the richer for it, they are all the richer for it.

Let's get cerebral for a moment. The following are five basic rules to live by for businesses:

1. Harm principle: businesses should avoid causing unwarranted harm.
2. Fairness principle: businesses should be fair in all of their practices.
3. Human rights principle: businesses should respect human rights.
4. Autonomy principle: businesses should not infringe on the rationally reflective choices of people (i.e., it's their decision; let them make it).

5. Veracity principle: businesses should not be deceptive in their practices.

These principles apply not only to a business's relationships and dealings with its customers and clients but also with its employees. In fact, those employee relationships are the most important of all. Without ethics there, the entire business is built on sand and will not last.

Johnson & Johnson, the famous pharmaceutical and health products corporation, publishes a succinct, on-the-money credo expressing its *internal* moral principles:

> We are responsible to our employees, the men and women who work with us throughout the world. Everyone must be considered as an individual. We must respect their dignity and recognize their merit. They must have a sense of security in their jobs. Compensation must be fair and adequate, and working conditions clean, orderly and safe. We must be mindful of ways to help our employees fulfill their family responsibilities.[53]

But remember, employees, too, have an ethical responsibility to the clients and customers and—even though they might not always think so—to the company that employs them. They need to be honest and forthright in everything they do as representatives of their company.

Famed investor Warren Buffett explains the strict ethical

---

53 "Working Here," Johnson & Johnson, Inc., June 27, 2011, http://www.jnj-canada.com/working-here.aspx.

codes within his companies: "I want employees to ask themselves whether they are willing to have any contemplated act **95** appear on the front page of their local paper the next day, to be read by their spouses, friends, and children. . . . If they follow this test, they need not fear my other message to them: lose money for the firm, and I will be understanding; lose a shred of reputation for the firm, and I will be ruthless."[54]

Well said.

Yet even Buffett faced an ethics challenge in spring 2011, when it was revealed that David Sokol, a Buffett lieutenant and possible Berkshire Hathaway successor to the man himself, had purchased thousands of shares in a chemical company he then recommended Berkshire buy. Sokol benefited financially but resigned his position with Berkshire when the details became public. Was it insider trading? The SEC is looking into the whole matter, and Buffett has chastised his former golden boy.[55]

So let's get cerebral again. The concept of ethics seems simple, but it's not. Just ask Buffett and Sokol.

Some people immediately think it has to do with what their feelings tell them is right or wrong. Seems logical. But relying on feelings to determine right or wrong is misguided because feelings—subjective and often overly emotional or irrational—can actually lead us to resist the right or embrace

---

54 Dominic Rushe, "Warren Buffett Admits 'I Made a Big Mistake' over David Sokol's Purchase of Lubrizol Shares," *Guardian*, April 30, 2011, http://www.guardian.co.uk/business/2011/apr/30/warren-buffett-big-mistake-david-sokol-lubrizol.

55 Ibid.

the wrong. Feelings can be unethical. Think of all the harm and damage that could be done if someone relied on feelings alone to determine what was right. For example, an employee may *feel* that she's justified in stealing office supplies because her boss didn't grant her the raise she requested. But that doesn't make the theft right.

So maybe ethics has to do with religious beliefs. In many ways, yes. Virtually all major religions are based on ethics and propose ethical rules—the Ten Commandments, treating your neighbor as yourself, and the like. The Bible, the Talmud, and the Koran are all bursting with passages about right and wrong. But religion does not encompass ethics. Ethics is more than religion. The atheist, too, should behave in an ethical manner. And of course, think of the harm and damage that has been done in the name of religion.

So is ethics something legal, something required by law? Laws can and should be just and fair and promote ethical behavior. But they don't always, of course. The Jim Crow laws in the South didn't. Statutes legalizing slavery didn't. The Nazis legally outlawed Jews. Does Sharia (Islamic law) always match a Christian's notion of ethics?

Maybe ethics simply means doing what society accepts. Oftentimes, sure. But again, that definition is too narrow, too limiting. Think of what some societies in the world accept—subjugation of women, religious intolerance, child labor. Accepted, yes. Ethical, no. Besides, societies, especially those that are the most free, are a tumultuous, dynamic mix of accepted and unaccepted. Much is not black-and-white; some is not ethical.

What, then, is ethics? Let's ask the Markkula Center for Applied Ethics at Santa Clara University in California, an organization that exists to help people and corporations figure out how best to live ethically and help create and maintain an ethical world. As the center explains it:

> Ethics is two things. First, ethics refers to well-founded standards of right and wrong that prescribe what humans ought to do, usually in terms of rights, obligations, benefits to society, fairness, or specific virtues. Ethics, for example, refers to those standards that impose the reasonable obligations to refrain from rape, stealing, murder, assault, slander, and fraud. Ethical standards also include those that enjoin virtues of honesty, compassion, and loyalty. And, ethical standards include standards relating to rights, such as the right to life, the right to freedom from injury, and the right to privacy. . . .
>
> Secondly, ethics refers to the study and development of one's ethical standards. . . . [F]eelings, laws, and social norms can deviate from what is ethical. So it is necessary to constantly examine one's standards to ensure that they are reasonable and well-founded. Ethics also means, then, the continuous effort of studying our own moral beliefs and our moral conduct, and striving to ensure that we, and the institutions we help to shape, live up to standards that are reasonable and solidly-based.[56]

---

56 Manuel Velasquez, Claire Andre, Thomas Shanks, S. J., and Michael J. Meyer, "What Is Ethics?" Markkula Center for Applied Ethics, 2010, http://www.scu. edu/ethics/practicing/decision/whatisethics.html.

Well, that's a little formal, of course, but we can all nod and smile as we read it. It's all true, we say to ourselves. But that doesn't mean it's easy. What about an ethical dilemma—a situation in which guiding moral principles cannot determine which course of action is right or wrong? Civil disobedience? White lies? A Sophie's choice? Whistle-blowers? It's enough to give you a headache.

Yet it always comes back to something inside—that part of you that knows what's right, knows what's moral, knows what's true. Then comes the toughest part: putting your ethics, your morals, into practice. Henry Ford did it. Sojourner Truth did it. Dave Steward did it.

They did the fearless, crazy thing. They did the right thing.

6

THINKING BIG

It's much easier for me to make major life, multimillion-dollar decisions than it is to decide on a carpet for my front porch. That's the truth.

—OPRAH WINFREY

Expand your horizons, shoot for the moon, dare to be great. Sometimes choices and decisions are fearless and crazy simply because they're the biggest and boldest. Too often we set our sights too low. We're realistic; we're embracing the possible. But if everyone always thought that way, the human race would be but an afterthought in the story of the universe. Instead—at least in our hopes and dreams—we are the center of that universe. Because we think big and aren't afraid to admit it.

100 Ultimate Train Set

Warren Buffett likes railroads, so in early 2010, he bought one: Burlington Northern Santa Fe (BNSF), the second-largest railroad in the country, behind Union Pacific. The tab? A mere $34 billion. Talk about thinking big. In fact, the *Wall Street Journal* reported, "Everything about this deal is big—from the price tag (Buffett's largest ever) to the scale of the company's business."[57]

The most famous investor now or ever, Warren Buffett is chairman and CEO of Berkshire Hathaway, a company made up of many other companies, which he found decades ago and is worth billions now. Buffett is the third-richest man in the world, behind Mexican telecom mogul Carlos Slim and Microsoft's Bill Gates, Buffett's close friend, bridge partner, and Berkshire board member.

Why a railroad? True to form, Buffett was quick with a quip when asked this question at the time of the sale's announcement: "This is all happening because my father didn't buy me a train set as a kid."[58]

Buffett is an old-school investor, looking for stability and sizing up management. And he invests in businesses and industries he knows or can figure out. He has never been

---

57 Michael Corkery, "Just How Big Is Buffett's Burlington Northern Bet?" *Wall Street Journal*, November 3, 2009, http://blogs.wsj.com/deals/2009/11/03/how-big-is-buffetts-railroad-bet.

58 Michael J. de la Merced and Andrew Ross Sorkin, "Buffet Bets Big on Railroads' Future," *New York Times*, November 3, 2009, http://www.nytimes.com/2009/11/04/business/04deal.html.

comfortable with tech stocks and more or less sat out the tech boom of the late 1990s. When that boom became a bust, he was vindicated but did little crowing. He was too busy running his company.

Railroads, too, are old school, an old-fashioned form of transportation, with clunky, rusty machinery and infrastructure constantly in need of attention. Yet Buffett had been attracted to trains for years, investing in Union Pacific and Norfolk Southern, as well as BNSF. Now that he has bought up all the outstanding shares of BNSF, that railroad is his. The following are just a few of the reasons Buffett took a rider on the rails:

- In recent years, railroads have modernized, with more efficient trains, fewer employees, and better bottom lines.
- Rail transport accounts for 43 percent of the freight hauled across the United States. BNSF has 32,000 route miles; the railroad has 220,000 freight cars clanking across the land at any given moment.
- BNSF is the result of mergers and acquisitions with 390 different rail companies over the past 150 years. It has approximately 40,000 employees.
- BNSF is the largest rail transporter of coal and grain. Each year it hauls enough coal to supply one out of every ten U.S. homes.
- Railroads are four times more fuel efficient than trucks. In 2010, BNSF moved each ton of freight it carried a record 500 miles per single gallon of diesel fuel. Although American railroads move 43 percent of our

nation's freight, they account for just 2.2 percent of all transportation-related greenhouse gases.

➡ Railroad freight loads are forecasted to nearly double by 2035.

Very attractive indeed, but there's one more reason Buffett stepped in and made the buy: it was, he said, "an all-in wager on the economic future of the United States."[59] The Great Recession was still great in late 2009, but Buffett wanted to let the world know that he saw much better days ahead, and railroads will help us get to those days sooner rather than later.

As he so often does when making a deal, Buffett acted quickly and informally. He traveled to Burlington's Fort Worth headquarters, liked what he saw of the operation and, most important, its management, and made his offer. Burlington shareholders were ecstatic; the company's stock jumped up immediately by 28 percent to $97 a share.

Berkshire's financials for 2010 showed that the elephant deal was already proving to be a good one. Owning BNSF increases Berkshire's normal-year earning power by nearly 40 percent pretax and 30 percent after tax. The company has already replenished the $22 billion in cash it spent to buy the railroad. In early 2011, Berkshire announced it had collected $2.5 billion in BNSF stock dividends in its first 13 months of ownership.

So it looks like Buffett's all-in wager is a winner. It was a fearless and crazy bet by the very nature of its incredible size

---

59 "Buffett Buying Burlington Northern Railroad," MSNBC.com, November 3, 2009, http://www.msnbc.msn.com/id/33599744/ns/business-us_business/t/buffett-buying-burlington-northern-railroad.

and scope. Buffett is never content to sit on his hands and his cash. But this acquisition, an entire railroad, was the grand- 103 daddy of them all. With a big dealer such as Buffett, the only question left to ask is what will he do next?

Face Time

The 2010 Oscar-nominated movie *The Social Network* didn't do him any favors, but Mark Zuckerberg seems to have bounced back nicely. He seems to be well on his way to conquering the world.

Okay, that may be a bit of a stretch, but Zuckerberg certainly does think big. His amazing social network creation, Facebook, has 600 million members worldwide and counting. While its overall reach continues to grow by leaps and bounds, its sophistication, applications, and uses continue to expand as well. And now it's even cited as a powerful tool for social and cultural change and revolution, bringing communication and access to many millions very quickly.

If that isn't enough, Mark Zuckerberg was named *Time* magazine's 2010 Person of the Year, and *Vanity Fair* magazine put him at number one on its 2010 list of the "100 most influential people of the Information Age."[60] Quite a load for a kid in his twenties.

---

60 See Lev Grossman, "Person of the Year 2010," *Time*, December 15, 2010, http://www.time.com/time/specials/packages/article/0,28804,2036683_2037183_2037185,00.html; and Alan Deutschman, Peter Newcomb, Richard Siklos, Duff McDonald, and Jessica Flint, "The Vanity Fair 100," *Vanity Fair*, October 2010, http://www.vanityfair.com/business/features/2010/10/the-vf-100-201010?currentPage=1.

It seems like it has been around forever, but Facebook was founded not that long ago, in 2004 at Harvard by Zuckerberg and classmates Dustin Moskovitz, Eduardo Saverin, and Chris Hughes. When he first showed up at Harvard, Zuckerberg already had a reputation as a "programming prodigy," a euphemism for "hacker." In his sophomore year, he wrote a program he called CourseMatch, which allowed users to make class selection decisions based on the choices of other students and helped them form study groups. A short time later, he created a different program he initially called Facemash that let students select the best-looking person from a choice of photos.

According to Zuckerberg's roommate at the time, Arie Hasit, "He built the site for fun. We had books called Face Books, which included the names and pictures of everyone who lived in the student dorms. At first, he built a site and placed two pictures, or pictures of two males and two females. Visitors to the site had to choose who was 'hotter' and according to the votes there would be a ranking." [61]

The site went up over a weekend, but by Monday morning, the college shut it down because its popularity had overwhelmed Harvard's server and prevented students from accessing the web. In addition, many students complained that their photos were being used without permission. Zuckerberg apologized publicly, and the student

---

61 Guy Grimland, "Facebook Founder's Roommate Recounts Creation of Internet Giant," Haretz.com, October 5, 2009, http://www.haaretz.com/news/facebook-founder-s-roommate-recounts-creation-of-internet-giant-1.275748.

paper ran articles stating that his site was "completely improper."[62]

At the time of Zuckerberg's "fun" site, however, students had already been requesting that the university develop a website that would include similar photos and contact details to be part of the college's computer network. According to Hasit, "Mark heard these pleas and decided that if the university won't do something about it, he will, and he would build a site that would be even better than what the university had planned."[63]

Zuckerberg launched Facebook from his Harvard dorm room on February 4, 2004. It started off as just a Harvard thing until Zuckerberg realized its potential and launched an aggressive plan to expand to other schools. With the help of roommate Dustin Moskovitz, he took Facebook to Stanford, Dartmouth, Columbia, New York University, Cornell, Brown, Yale, and several other schools that had social contacts with Harvard.

Zuckerberg was having the time of his young life. He moved to Palo Alto, California, along with Moskovitz and some other friends. They leased a small house that served as an office. Over the summer of 2004, Zuckerberg met Peter Thiel, who invested in the company, and Facebook soon had its first real headquarters.

Several major corporations made offers for the company as its growth and influence continued to make news. Zuckerberg could have taken the money and run, but he saw

---

62 Ibid.

63 Ibid.

something bigger in all this. "It's not because of the amount of money," he explained in a 2007 interview. "For me and my colleagues, the most important thing is that we create an open information flow for people. Having media corporations owned by conglomerates is just not an attractive idea to me."[64]

Zuckerberg and those colleagues of his may have relocated to California, but there was trouble back at Harvard. Harvard students Cameron Winklevoss, his twin Tyler Winklevoss, and Divya Narendra accused Zuckerberg of intentionally making them believe he would help them build a social network called HarvardConnection.com (later called ConnectU). Instead, they claim, he spent his time working up Facebook. They filed a lawsuit in 2004, but it was dismissed on a technicality on March 28, 2007. It was refiled soon thereafter in federal court in Boston. Facebook and Zuckerberg countersued.

On June 25, 2008, the case settled, and Facebook agreed to transfer more than 1.2 million common shares and pay $20 million in cash to the Winklevoss group. The battle with the twins is the central plot of *The Social Network*. But the Winklevosses weren't satisfied with the $20 million, feeling they should have gotten much more in light of Facebook's amazing growth. They sued again, claiming they were misled about the value of Facebook. In April 2011, the courts denied them, ruling that the first settlement was fine and fair. The

---

64 "Face-to-Face with Mark Zuckerberg '02," *Lion's Eye*, Phillips Exeter Academy, January 24, 2007, http://www.exeter.edu/news_and_events/news_events_5594.aspx.

twins dropped their appeal of that ruling and quickly filed a new lawsuit. The legal battle continues. At least the lawyers are smiling.[65]

Lawsuits, movies, whatever—Facebook's growth and influence seem to have no bounds. Goldman Sachs invested in January 2011 and placed the company's valuation at $50 billion. A couple of months later, Russian investment bank Otkritie said Facebook was worth $76.4 billion. How high can it go? Is this another speculation bubble? As always, time will tell.

In the meantime, Zuckerberg has been doing all the right things. He has wisely distanced himself and his company from all of the revolution turmoil in the Mideast and Africa. Facebook is undoubtedly a significant tool for communication and change, and Zuckerberg refuses to take sides or promote an agenda in other cultures. Like TV, radio, and print, Facebook may spread the news, but it doesn't, and shouldn't, make the news.

Zuckerberg did make news on the philanthropic front in 2010 when he founded the Startup: Education foundation. On September 22 of that year, the media buzzed with reports that Zuckerberg had arranged to donate $100 million to Newark Public Schools, the public school system of Newark, New Jersey. Critics and cynics saw the donation and its timing as PR ploys, with the release of *The Social Network* and its unflattering portrayal of Zuckerberg at hand.

---

65 Charles Arthur, "Facebook Paid Up to $65m to Founder Mark Zuckerberg's Ex-classmates," guardian.co.uk, February 12, 2009, http://www.guardian.co.uk/technology/2009/feb/12/facebook-mark-zuckerberg-ex-classmates.

But Zuckerberg responded immediately: "The thing that I was most sensitive about with the movie timing was I didn't want the press about *The Social Network* movie to get conflated with the Newark project. I was thinking about doing this anonymously just so that the two things could be kept separate."[66]

Really? Apparently so, because both Newark mayor Cory Booker and New Jersey governor Chris Christie came to Zuckerberg's defense and said they had to convince Zuckerberg's team not to make the donation anonymously. They saw it as a big spotlight moment for their communities and schools. The cynics backed off.

A few months later, in December 2010, Zuckerberg released a statement that he had become a signatory of the Giving Pledge, the philanthropic effort spearheaded by two other big thinkers, Bill Gates and Warren Buffett.[67] Signatories to the pledge agree to leave most or all of their accumulated fortunes to charity. By putting his name on the dotted line, Zuckerberg is demonstrating once again that he is ready for prime time, ready to join the big boys. Thinking big, always.

What were you thinking about at age 30?

---

66 Mike Isaac, "Zuckerberg Pressured to Announce $100 Million Donation to Newark," *Forbes*, September 24, 2010, http://www.forbes.com/sites/velocity/2010/09/24/zuckerberg-pressured-to-announce-100-million-donation-to-newark/.

67 Joshua Norman, "Mark Zuckerberg Pledges Most of $6 Billion Fortune to Charity," CBS News.com, December 9, 2010, http://www.cbsnews.com/8301-503983_162-20025110-503983.html.

A Leap of Faith

On October 28, 1958, Angelo Giuseppe Roncalli officially joined a select group in history. On that date, Roncalli, the son of sharecroppers from a small country village in the Italian province of Bergamo, was elected the 261st Pope of the Catholic Church and Sovereign of Vatican City.

Cardinal Roncalli's election was a surprise to all, even him. In fact, he traveled to the conclave of cardinals—the meeting to vote for the new pope—with a return train ticket in his pocket. He certainly didn't think he'd be staying on—for the rest of his life, as it turned out.

Because he was older—76 the day he got the job—most assumed he'd be a mere stopgap pope, filling the office for a few short years until the cardinals could get the man they really wanted to be pope—Giovanni Montini, Archbishop of Milan (who could not become a pope at the time because he had not yet been made a cardinal). And they were right: Roncalli served less than five years, dying in June 1963, and shortly thereafter, Montini was elected and became Pope Paul VI.

But during the five years of his reign, Roncalli—Pope John XXIII—turned the Roman Catholic Church inside out and upside down. The sharecroppers' son may have been a simple, friendly man, but he was a big thinker as well.

He was fearless and crazy from the beginning, starting with the selection of his papal name. The name John hadn't been chosen by a pope for more than 500 years, primarily because the last Pope John was considered an "antipope" after

the Western Schism split the Catholic Church. Nonetheless,
110 Roncalli chose John, "a name sweet to us because it is the
name of our father, dear to me because it is the name of the
humble parish church where I was baptized."[68]

Within weeks of his coronation, Pope John XXIII was
turning heads and making headlines. On Christmas Day
1958, he became the first pope since 1870 to make pastoral
visits in his diocese of Rome. He visited two hospitals in the
city, bringing comfort to the sick, including children with
polio. The next day, he practiced another of Jesus' beatitudes,
visiting inmates at Rome's Regina Coeli prison. "You could
not come to me," he told the prisoners. "So I came to you."[69]

These good works created a sensation, and the world had
begun to discover that this pope named John was something
special.

And then he did something so special, so extraordinary,
that his place in history was secured: just three months after
his election, he called for an ecumenical council, a gathering
of all the church's bishops to meet and decide major issues of
faith, tradition, and policy. Pope John XXIII explained why
he called the council in simple terms: it was time to open the
windows of the church and let in a little fresh air.

The last ecumenical council had been called a century
earlier and was known as the First Council of the Vatican,

---

68 "I Chose John," *Time* magazine, November 10, 1958, http://www.time.com/
time/magazine/article/0,9171,938062-3,00.html.

69 Peter Hebblethwaite, *Pope John XXIII: Shepherd of the Modern World* (Garden
City, NY: Doubleday Religious Publishing, 1987), 303.

or Vatican I. Among the decisions made then were how to define the pope's primacy in church governance and the establishment of his infallibility. 111

John XXIII's ecumenical council would be known forever as the Second Council of the Vatican, or Vatican II. It lasted from October 1962 until December 1965. It is still discussed and debated, praised and pilloried by Catholics throughout the world. It shook up the Roman Catholic Church, causing rumblings felt to this day.

For starters, many of Vatican II's proceedings were open to the laity and even non-Catholic observers—all part of the open windows the pope promoted. In general, Vatican II called for a modernization of many church practices in order to foster a dialogue with the world and better spread the good news of the Gospel. One of the most visible changes was the church's allowing the celebration of the Mass in the vernacular (i.e., current languages such as English, Spanish, and French, depending on the country) instead of exclusively in Latin.

The role of the laity (nonordained persons) in the procedures and traditions of the church was greatly expanded. Women could enter the sacristy. Laymen and laywomen could assist with Communion.

Most important of all, Vatican II opened the door (as well as the windows) to disagreement and even dissension within the church, from both laity and clergy. Today many Catholics do not hesitate to question major church doctrine, including male-only priesthood, clerical celibacy, and pro-life rigidity.

Not surprisingly, there has been a backlash against the "liberal" Vatican II changes, with many Catholics feeling the church has gone overboard in its embrace of modernity. They not only want a return to the Latin Mass, they want the guitars and tambourines put away as well.

The Roman Catholic Church continues to struggle with the decisions of Vatican II. Unfortunately, the man who started it all, Pope John XXIII, died about eight months after the council began. His predecessor, Paul VI, presided over Vatican II from then on until its conclusion.

But Pope John knew he was stirring things up. He knew he was launching something big, something monumental in church history. He knew an open window lets in cold and wind as well as heat and light. He knew some would call him fearless; others would call him crazy.

But this was his moment and the church's. He would be proud.

The Original Greeter

If you're of a certain age, you certainly remember Ben Franklin stores—five-and-dimes they called them—which had just about everything and anything you could need. It was a Ben Franklin store in Newport, Arkansas, that set a young Oklahoma man on the path to retail history. Fresh from service in the Army during World War II, young Sam Walton purchased that franchise store with the help of a $20,000 loan from his father and $5,000 he'd saved while in the service. Pretty big money for a man in his mid-twenties in the mid-1940s. It was just the beginning.

When he bought that store, it was generating about $72,000

a year in annual sales. Five years later, Walton had that number up to $250,000. The building's landlord liked what he saw and refused to renew Walton's lease even though he was getting a princely 5 percent of Walton's sales. He wanted the business for himself. Walton sold the store's inventory to the landlord and moved on to greener and bigger pastures.

Walton then purchased a store from Luther Harrison in Bentonville, Arkansas, and renamed it Walton's 5&10. The 2,900 citizens of Bentonville certainly didn't realize it then, but their Ozark Mountain town had just become the headquarters of what would become the largest retailer in the world. By 1962, Walton and his brother Bud owned 16 variety stores—15 of them Ben Franklins in Arkansas, Missouri, and Kansas.

But it was time for another of Walton's many fearless career decisions: leave the franchise empire and create an empire of his own. He opened the first Walmart store in Rogers, Arkansas, on July 2, 1962. In that store and those that quickly followed, he and his team were determined to stock their shelves with American goods and sought out U.S. manufacturers whose merchandise was cheap enough to beat foreign competition. The strategy of pressuring suppliers for low and even the lowest prices has become a Walmart retailing hallmark. Yet nothing Walton or his stores did was revolutionary; they just did it better. "I probably have traveled and walked into more variety stores than anybody in America," said Walton. "I am just trying to get ideas, any kind of ideas that will help our company. Most of us don't invent ideas. We take the best ideas from someone else."[70]

---

70 Barbara Farfan, "Quotations from Sam Walton," About.com, http://retailindustry
.about.com/od/frontlinemanagement/a/walmartsamwaltonquotesretailing.htm.

The growth was nonstop. By 1967, there were 24 Walmart stores throughout Arkansas. By 1975, there were 125 stores in nine states, 7,500 employees, and $340 million in sales. Then came the acquisitions—Mohr-Value stores in 1977 and Hutcheson Shoe Company in 1978. Walmart stores now included pharmacies, jewelry stores, and auto service centers. By 1979, Walton's empire was 276 stores strong, employing 21,000 workers. Sales topped $1.24 billion.

But the world hadn't seen anything yet. The amazing growth continued and has yet to stop. The folksy yet brilliant Sam Walton became a living legend in the retail business. The success formula—name brands at low prices—was matched by effective internal policies as well. After taking the company public in 1970, Walton introduced his "profit sharing plan" for company employees and offered workers stock options and store discounts. Such perks are common today but were rare in the early 1970s.[71]

Walton continually praised and thanked those who worked for him and with him. "Appreciate everything your associates do for the business," he advised his managers. "Nothing else can quite substitute for a few well-chosen, well-timed, sincere words of praise. They're absolutely free and worth a fortune."[72]

In his 1992 autobiography, *Sam Walton: Made in America*,

---

71 Amanda Galiano, "Sam Walton & Wal-mart," About.com, http://littlerock. about.com/cs/homeliving/a/aasamwalton.htm.

72 Ben Brinkopf, "Ten Rules of Success from Sam Walton," The Leadership Institute at Harvard College, January 25, 2011, http://harvardleadership.wordpress. com/2011/01/25/ten-rules-of-success-from-sam-walton/.

he listed his 10 commandments for business, basic tenets
that are appropriate in any industry in any era:

1. Commit to your business.
2. Share your profits with all your associates, and treat
   them as partners.
3. Motivate your partners.
4. Communicate everything you possibly can to your
   partners.
5. Appreciate everything your associates do for the
   business.
6. Celebrate your successes.
7. Listen to everyone in your company.
8. Exceed your customers' expectations.
9. Control your expenses better than your
   competition.
10. Swim upstream.[73]

But big often means controversy, and Walton and his
stores have certainly had their share. The ongoing criticism is,
of course, that when a giant Walmart or Sam's Club (Walton's
membership-based discount warehouse stores) comes into a
community, the local mom-and-pop stores can't compete
and soon wither and die. Many regard Walmart as the enemy
of Main Street.

In recent years, there has been a seemingly endless pro-
cession of lawsuits from employees or former employees

---

73 Sam Walton, *Sam Walton: Made in America* (New York: Bantam, 1993),
314–317.

claiming workplace discrimination because of race or gender. In June 2011, the U.S. Supreme Court unanimously ruled that a gender discrimination lawsuit against Walmart cannot go on as a class action in its current form. If the court had not ruled with Walmart, the suit would have been the largest discrimination case in U.S. history, with as many as 1.5 million female plaintiffs.[74] Even Walmart's legal dealings are big. Yet had Sam Walton been alive to witness such courtroom disputes, he certainly would have been sad. The legal wrangling seems to fly in the face of his 10 commandments.

Sam Walton received the Presidential Medal of Freedom from President George H. W. Bush in March 1992. A few short weeks later, he was dead, a victim of multiple myeloma. At the time of his death, there were 1,960 Walmart stores. He left his ownership in the company to his wife and children. Family members continue to hold key positions in the company and make key strategic decisions. Two of those recent decisions are crucial to the ongoing growth and success of the corporation.

First, Walmart, the biggest of the big, is thinking small. It is creating mini-Walmart stores, called Walmart Express, to more easily reach both urban and rural customers and compete against smaller discount chains such as Dollar Stores. Fittingly, the first Walmart Express opened in June 2011 in Arkansas. Similarly, the company is developing a network of small, stand-alone grocery stores suitable for congested city neighborhoods.

---

74 Nina Totenberg, "Supreme Court Limits Walmart Discrimination Case," NPR, June 20, 2011, http://www.npr.org/2011/06/20/137296721/supreme-court-limits-wal-mart-discrimination-case.

Second, through Walmart Stores Inc., the Walton family has been aggressively buying back shares of the corpora- tion with the goal of soon owning more than 50 percent of the common stock.[75] Yes, the company will still be publicly traded, but it will also be a family business once again—just like when Sam started small but with a big, crazy dream all those decades ago in Arkansas.

■ ■ ■

➡ MY TAKE

Making business deals—from the biggest ones that take months to finalize and involve teams of lawyers, to the smallest ones that are sealed with a handshake after a 10-minute chat—is an art. When you're accomplished at that art, you put together deals in which all parties involved walk away with a win.

But let's be clear on what we mean by a *win*.

Many people confuse getting what they want with winning. Just because *you* get what *you* want from a deal doesn't mean you won. Sometimes it does but not always. It's shortsighted to assume that having what you want and winning are one and the same. Among other things, it can actually hinder future deals because you walk out of a situation without realizing its full potential.

If you create a truly good deal, you're going to want to do the same thing over and over again. If you don't walk away from a final agreement confident that both you and the other

---

75 "$15 Billion Buyback to Strengthen Family's Control of Walmart," Bloomberg News, June 5, 2011.

118 parties will want to work together again, your deal probably wasn't as good as you thought. A big deal should spawn even bigger deals.

So how do you go about creating a good deal? First, you have to be ready to ask for more than what you need or want out of the arrangement. Although there might be intangibles at work, you should essentially walk into a negotiation ready to ask for commitments, orders, or referrals from your client (or potential client). It takes more time and money to gain a *new* client or a *new* investor than to keep one, so you should always be working on repeat business with your existing clients. If you have established a positive, productive relationship with a client, you should never hesitate to ask for repeat business.

It may sound obvious, but most people just don't do it. They're scared; they can't stand the thought of being rejected. But if you don't ask, you'll never know. And you could be shutting yourself off from what might be a very profitable deal and an ongoing, mutually beneficial relationship. In my life-wealth plan, asking for repeat business is what I call no-nonsense networking.

You have to be fearless and ask the obvious but often tough questions: "How do you want to do business with me so we can make more money together?" "Would you like to develop another deal together to make more money?" You'll express yourself better than that, of course, but those are the underlying messages.

There is a strategic way to ask for another order or another deal. Take yourself out of the picture, and think about what you need to do to make your potential partners more successful and richer. Turn the situation around and see it from *their* perspective. What can you do to help them meet *their* goals? 119

Think about giving your potential partners your formula. Share whatever it is that made you and your business successful. If you know your product is strong enough, and you know how to integrate your product into what they want or need, then help your partners maneuver through the deal so that they can appreciate your value and see what you bring to the table—to *their* table.

You have to make small deals to learn how to make big deals. Small deals create big deals. Small deals can help you gain confidence in what you're doing and also nurture other people's confidence in you. You have to crawl before you can walk. But that doesn't mean you have to crawl forever. People often think they're settling for less, not attaining their potential, or cheating themselves because they seem mired in small deals and routine negotiations. But remember, it's the small ones that lead to the big one. Warren Buffett, Mark Zuckerberg, Pope John XXIII, and Sam Walton didn't start out making headlines. They crawled before they could walk.

The following are some basic steps to becoming an artist of the deal—whether you're negotiating for a railroad or a rental car, whether you're acting on behalf of a worldwide organization or just for your own sole proprietorship. As you go through the steps, remember my life-wealth plan and its components: vision, planning, execution, marketing, networking, and dealing with the unknown.

• **STEP 1: Know your product.** When I had just started my financial services business, I wanted to be the most knowledgeable person ever in the investment field. To me, that seemed like the most important goal, the best pathway to incredible success. But there were more than 15,000 mutual funds at that time—more than 15,000 investment possibilities—and I had only two days to learn about them all before my first client meeting. My goal seemed an impossible one.

So instead of trying to perform the impossible—become familiar and comfortable with 15,000 funds—I opted for the possible. I continued my work developing five portfolios of funds that focused on the financial interests and needs of specific types of clients: individuals, families, and corporations. Each portfolio included about five appropriate mutual funds that I had researched thoroughly and knew like the back of my hand.

The mix of funds in each portfolio was based on the various risk factors that fit a specific investment personality. The portfolio names indicated what was inside: Aggressive, Moderate Aggressive, Moderate, Moderate Conservative, and Conservative.

The Aggressive model, for example, was geared primarily toward young people just starting out in their investing life. They have time to go for the riskier growth stocks that often move up quickly but can drop just as quickly. Young investors can ride out the price swings and do quite well in the long run.

The Conservative model, on the other hand, was just the opposite. It was designed for those who were already wealthy and wanted to keep their money secure, perhaps letting it grow a bit faster than inflation but always protecting the principal. These investors are primarily older, established, 121 and eager to "conserve" what they have worked so hard and long to earn.

Some of the same funds would be part of the mix in several of my portfolios. For example, a particular emerging markets fund—often a somewhat risky investment—might be a big piece of the Aggressive portfolio but a much smaller piece in the Conservative.

For each of the various portfolio models, I had the data, the hypotheticals, and the research all mapped out, ready to support my recommendation. For each of the mutual funds within a given portfolio, I had fund company histories, track records, philosophies, sales strategies, and executive bios. I got to know personally the key management and sales personnel at each company.

By moving my clients into these few targeted, diversified portfolios, I was able to send a steady, significant stream of orders to these fund companies that I now knew so well and trusted implicitly. In return, I, my company, and—most important—my clients received excellent service and extra incentives from these companies. And by combining individual client investments into a particular company, we reduced the cost of the investment, the fees. For example, if a person invests $50,000 in a company, he or she could be charged a quarterly fee, a small percentage of the value. Pool the investments of several individuals to more than $100,000, and you might avoid fees altogether.

By working tirelessly with clients and fund companies to create products I knew and believed in, I was able to close

the deal. Many deals, many times. And *create* is the key word,
because I was practicing the art of the deal.

• **STEP 2: Show the opportunity.** Early in my career, I wanted to build a solid track record to use as leverage when I approached other companies. I wanted to be able to use what I had already achieved as a means of attracting others to become a part of my product mix. By performing and being a top advisor for other companies, I could show the new ones hard data, a record of success. I could convince them with facts that the right financial support and resources would allow me to do what I had done in the past. I could essentially transfer my experience and skills to benefit their company.

I would put my track record on paper and present a clear and specific execution plan. I would give them straightforward insight into my vision and goals. They would consider me an excellent *in*trepreneur—someone who is on the inside as an employee of theirs but who has the latitude, instincts, and skills to act as an *en*trepreneur on their behalf. My dealmaking past had become my portfolio for the future.

Relationship management is the key to showing them who you are, what you can do, and how it will benefit everyone involved. You learn about them; they learn about you. Both must agree that there's synergy; a professional relationship is forged. Then handshakes happen and agreements are signed.

Frequently, my deals close quickly and easily because people already know they want to do business with me. If you create a strong enough brand and a strong enough reputation, people will want to be part of what you do and who you are. That's the magic Warren Buffett possesses. When he extends his hand, you take it (with a big grin on your face). Have the solid brand and the stellar reputation, and people 123 will clamor to close the deal—they see profits in their future.

• **STEP 3: Get buy-in on your vision.** One of my most difficult deals, one I mentioned previously, involved developing a partnership to acquire the film, TV, and digital rights for the works of author Omar Tyree. Mainly because Tyree had been a go-it-alone soldier for so many years, it was difficult to bring about the deal. For him, turning over the successful brand he had built for almost 20 years to someone else was hard to even imagine, let alone actually do. His best and only partner had been himself.

Even though he was hitting the wall in Hollywood, he still felt he was in control. It was a challenge for me, given my perspective and my interest, to try to explain to Tyree that the film biz was truly new territory for him, that he was involved in a new industry, and that whatever he might have thought, whatever illusion he might have had, he was not in control and could never be in total control. In Hollywood, the game is collaboration.

My challenge was to show him that he would continue to be involved in the projects, serving as an advisor. I had to convince him that he would benefit from his literary works being developed into other mediums. But at the same time, if he didn't give up some creative control, he would scuttle the possibility of agreement between the various parties, and the entire initiative would sink like a stone.

In effect, I had to convince my partner Omar Tyree that it was better to make a smaller amount of money being a part of a very big deal, benefiting many, than trying to make a bigger amount of money as part of a deal whose chances of success were slight. And that's the way it finally came together.

But before we got to that point, I had to address his personal concerns. In deal making, to get someone to buy into your vision, you must first understand theirs. Tyree wanted to ensure his family would always have money from his work, he wanted to gain stronger national exposure, and he wanted to diversify his income so he could do other projects he had always been passionate about. That was his three-part vision, with part one being the most important.

Our deal took all of this into account. In the end, we both had to give a little and yield a little. And we did that by seeing the world from the other's perspective. It's called understanding, and it's the key to deal making—big, small, or in between.

- **STEP 4: Be humble.** You have to be humble but firm to broker a deal effectively. There's a fine line between the two, particularly when you're dealing with people who have already attained a measure of success. They're used to the light shining on them; they're used to having it their way.

Always respect the positions of the other people involved in your negotiations, whether you truly want the deal or not. Again, it is only an offer, and their response is merely a response to that offer. It's the opening salvo and countersalvo. It's important to be fair and honest about the deal and to keep your intentions pure.

You need to let people know you have the wherewithal to perform the task you're charged with. You need to convey

that you put 100 percent effort behind everything you do. At
the same time, you must express genuine respect and appre- 125
ciation for what they do, what they have done, and who they
are—even if they're jerks. Because even a jerk can grow to
appreciate and respect you, and once that two-way street is
established, negotiations can begin and a deal can be struck.
Humility with backbone. It's a tricky combination to maintain, but it's absolutely crucial.

• **STEP 5: Finesse.** Almost every deal I do takes finesse. And
to my mind, finesse is where skill and natural ability meet.
This is where I get to have fun and allow my personality to
shine. I get to explore different angles and try the somewhat
weird and wacky—maybe even a bit of the fearless and crazy.
It's problem solving with a twist when, in the end, finesse
comes into play, the parties genuinely like each other, and all
sides look for ways to make sure the deal becomes a reality.
For the best wheeler-dealers, finesse comes naturally; they
don't even know they're doing it. If you're lucky, it works that
way for you as well. If not, develop it, let it flow, and have
fun trying it. Before you know it, you'll be finessing your
deals too.

• **STEP 6: Swagger.** Very much related to problem solving
with a twist, swagger is something you implement through
finesse, something that uses finesse as a tool. If finesse is
about problem solving and outside-the-box thinking, then
swagger is about having attitude without being pretentious
or arrogant. It's about knowing how good you are in business
and hinting at what you are capable of. Yet it's something

you possess, show, and use without ever compromising your integrity or sacrificing your general likability. Remember, arrogance and pretentiousness are rarely attractive in any context. In a business setting, though, it's swagger—a carefully pulled-off attitude—that lets people know your capabilities, whether they choose to use them or not.

Your swagger says that it really doesn't matter if the deal happens or not. Things will be fine; the sun will still come up tomorrow. You're giving off a vibe that says, no matter what, I'm still confident and secure. Your swagger says you're good at what you do and you know it. It also implies that there'll be many deals for you in the days and years ahead, and if this one happens, fine. If it doesn't happen, another will. If the people across the table decide not to partner with you, there'll soon be other people and other tables. Used effectively, your swagger will have those people all but begging you to seal the deal with them and smiling as they do so. Hit the right notes with your swagger, and you'll walk away with what you want. You'll be working and perfecting your life-wealth plan.

These steps are instinctual for some but can be learned and developed by others. For many, it takes practice to be able to react on the fly to whatever situation may come up and to take the offensive without people being offended or even realizing it's happening. In other words, it takes practice to have a negotiating style that doesn't seem practiced. Like everything else in life, the more you do it, the better you get at it.

Master the six steps outlined above, and you will have mastered the art of deal making. You will be the embodi- ment of life-wealth. Remember, though, that Rome wasn't built in a day, and neither is deal-making talent. You're very unlikely to land the deal of a lifetime right out of the box in your business career. You have to start small, pile up the minor successes, and throw in a mid-size deal or two, and next thing you know, they're writing you up in *Forbes* magazine. But you can't force it; you have to pace yourself. You have to stumble a few times, get back up, and go at it again. You need to keep both your successes and your failures in perspective, remembering that they are just stepping-stones along your lifetime of deal adventures. Work on the six steps above. Read them over from time to time. Quickly or eventually, you'll become a deal artist.

And remember, once you get good at it, aim high—just like those three billionaires and that pope.

7

BY DESIGN

People ignore design that ignores people.

—FRANK CHIMERO

Sometimes being fearless and crazy isn't about the decisions you make or the paths you take but about the things you create. It's about genius and ingenuity, insight and inspiration. Some amazing people among us (and I hope you're one) have that God-given something, that special gift that lets them see, feel, and create works of art—products that make our lives better and our spirits more fulfilled. They are the people who lift us—at least for a few precious moments—from our grinding earthbound existence to the heights of the angels.

130 His Own Devices

Consider the Apple iPad 2, introduced in March 2011. It's not that much different from its amazing predecessor, the iPad, the most buzzed-about e-device since Apple's iPhone (which, of course, was the most buzzed-about device since the iPod).

The first iPad sold more than 15 million copies in nine months, at a price of $500 or more, depending on how much power and how many bells and whistles it had. Its amazing success has led to a flood of other tablets, all of which are threatening to make the laptop computer as obsolete as the typewriter.

When you compare the iPad 2 to its iPad parent, you notice the obvious: it's one-third thinner, 15 percent lighter, and twice as fast. It also has front and back cameras, one of which is an HD video cam. All of that's important, but there's more: an optional screen cover that protects the screen and doubles as a stand to prop the iPad 2 upright—available in five different colors of polyurethane or five different colors of leather. When you open the screen cover, the iPad 2 powers up instantaneously, not within a few seconds like even the fastest PCs and the original iPad. There's a gyroscope too, which is needed for some advanced games. And of course, there are all those apps—65,000 and counting, plus another 290,000 iPhone apps that run at lower resolution on an iPad screen.

But those are just the facts. The iPad 2—and everything else that Apple has created or will create—is flat-out fun to see, fun to hold, and fun to use. There's something subjective, something visceral, about Apple's products that even Apple's detractors cannot deny. Apple's products are different; they're unique. They're well designed.

Consider the man behind those designs, the man who is the face and spirit of Apple: Steve Jobs. At the March 2011 unveiling of the iPad 2 in San Francisco, he suddenly walked out onto the stage, and the crowd gasped and then quickly cheered. The man himself, dressed in his trademark black turtleneck and jeans, was back. He got a standing ovation.

In January of 2011, he had announced his third medical leave of absence from Apple's helm, the result of his 2004 pancreatic cancer diagnosis. His health problems had raised questions about Apple's future without him. But here he was again—thin as ever—doing what he does so well: promoting his newest product, zinging the competition, exuding excitement and enthusiasm, and working the crowd. By the time he left the stage, Apple shares had jumped $3. Vintage Jobs, vintage Apple. Well timed and well executed. The entire event, just like Apple's products, was well designed.

In a fearless, crazy, and consistent way, Jobs and his company were like no others in the tech industry. Love 'em or hate 'em, you had to shake your head and admire them. Apple Inc. is the darling of Main Street as well as Wall Street. Its market capitalization has surpassed that of Microsoft, Google, and IBM. Many predict its share price will continue to climb from over $300 to $500 and beyond.

How did all this happen? Well, it's a familiar story and a crazy one.

Born in San Francisco in 1955, Steve Jobs set off on his tech path sometime between high school and college. Jobs frequented after-school lectures at the Hewlett-Packard Company in Palo Alto, California, working there over a summer with his future business associate Steve Wozniak.

132

After high school, Jobs enrolled in Reed College in Portland, Oregon. He dropped out after one semester but later pointed out that if he hadn't taken a class in calligraphy while there, "the Mac would have never had multiple typefaces or proportionally spaced fonts."[76]

In the fall of 1974, Jobs returned to California and took a job at video game producer Atari. He saved enough money to travel to India, where, like so many before him and since, he sought spiritual enlightenment. He took along a friend from Reed College, Daniel Kottke, who later would become the first Apple employee.

While in India, Jobs apparently did find the enlightenment he sought, even shaving his head and wearing traditional Indian clothing. He hadn't abandoned his old life for something new, however. Far from it. The Indian trip was merely preparation for the road ahead—in business in America.

Back home, Jobs returned to his old job at Atari. One of his first assignments was to create a circuit board for a game called Breakout. According to the Atari company founder, Nolan Bushnell, Atari had offered its game developers a $100 bonus for each chip in the Breakout board they could eliminate (i.e., make redundant). The idea was to streamline the game without losing power or functionality. Jobs took up the challenge, even though he didn't know how to eliminate

---

76 "You've Got to Do What You Love, Jobs Says," *Stanford University News*, June 14, 2005, http://news.stanford.edu/news/2005/june15/jobs-061505.html.

the chips. What he did know is someone who did—Steve Wozniak. He enlisted his old summer job buddy to help 133 him; the two would split the bonus money. To the amazement of everybody at Atari, Wozniak reduced the number of chips by 50, creating a design so tight that it was impossible to reproduce on an assembly line.[77]

A Jobs-Wozniak partnership was born. By 1976, the two of them and friend Ronald Wayne set about building Apple, a company that would assemble and sell computers. The three-fledgling entrepreneurs were lucky to get some funding from the then-semiretired Intel product marketing manager and engineer A. C. "Mike" Markkula. They were on their way.

In 1978, to help manage expansion, Apple recruited Mike Scott, an experienced manager from National Semiconductor. Scott served as CEO for several turbulent years and in 1983 was succeeded by John Sculley from Pepsi-Cola. Apparently the key to Jobs's recruiting pitch was a question he asked Sculley: "Do you want to sell sugar water for the rest of your life, or do you want to come with me and change the world?" Sculley opted for the latter.[78]

In 1984, Apple cemented its reputation for edginess with its now-famous "1984" Super Bowl television commercial. In the commercial, Apple introduced to the world the Macintosh computer, the first personal computer with a graphical user interface. Jobs himself had worked extensively

---

77 Steven Kent, *The Ultimate History of Video Games* (New York: Three Rivers Press, 2001), 71-73.

78 Andrew Leonard, "Do Penguins Eat Apples?" Salon.com, September 28, 1999, http://www.salon.com/technology/feature/1999/09/28/mac_linux/index.html.

on its development. The machine's simplicity and design were remarkable. The nickname "Mac" eventually became a household name. The term "user-friendly" was often used in the same sentence as "Mac."

As the face of Apple, Jobs could be inspirational and charismatic, but to many of his employees and coworkers, he was also erratic, arrogant, and aggressive. When sales slumped in late 1984 and early 1985, he was ousted by the Apple board led by John Sculley, the very man Jobs convinced to leave the sugar water industry.

Jobs was out but not down for long. He started another computer company, NeXT, whose hardware and software would be highly advanced technologically and marketed primarily to the scientific and academic fields. In fact, Jobs went as far as to describe one of the NeXT products, the NeXT-cube, as an "interpersonal" computer. In his opinion, the level of innovation it brought to the market was beyond what was already accessible via the "personal" computer models. The NeXTcube, Jobs believed, was the next step after "personal" computing, setting the basis for people to communicate and collaborate using computers and thereby overcoming the problems of "personal" computing. Indeed, at a time when most people were totally unaware of email (and those who were emailed in plain text), Jobs was busy demonstrating a new emailing system, NeXTMail, which was incorporated into the NeXT computer system and used, by Jobs at least, to demonstrate the "interpersonal"—bridging the communication gap between machines and people. NeXTMail was one of the first systems to allow people to send audio and graphic content within their emails.

But there was the bottom line—there's *always* the bottom line. The company sold only about 50,000 computers. Jobs ran the company with such an obsessive focus on perfection that nothing went smoothly; everyone and everything was strained. The company was broken into hardware and software divisions, and the hardware division was sold in 1993. The emphasis on NeXT software development continued for another three years until the rest of the company was put up for sale.

Enter Apple. Jobs's old company bought his new one, NeXT, for $429 million and, in the process, brought Jobs back to Apple. In a relatively short time, he was established as Apple's interim CEO after the directors lost confidence in then-CEO Gil Amelio. The boardroom coup was unexpected, but Jobs was in a position to take advantage of the company's failing profitability.

By March 1998, Jobs had developed a plan to return Apple to the black ink. He started out by terminating a number of projects that weren't working out. Although many Apple employees were subsequently terrified of losing their jobs, only a few people actually were let go as a result of his overhaul of the company. Apple and Jobs had established a reputation for being unafraid of ditching any initiative that wasn't panning out—in other words, cutting their losses and moving on to something better. One of those better things was the iMac, noted not only for its ease of use but for its sleek, elegant design. It looked as good as it worked. To Jobs, of course, performance and design went hand in hand.

And not just for computers. Back in 1986, Jobs had purchased the Graphics Group from Lucasfilm for $10 million. The company was intended to be a high-end graphics hardware developer. It called its flagship equipment the Pixar Image Computer, but sales were modest at best. Then Jobs struck a deal with Disney to produce computer-animated feature films. Pixar, as the company was now called, would make the movies; Disney would cofinance and distribute them.

Toy Story, the first film produced by the studio, was released in 1995 to critical acclaim and stellar box office receipts. Overnight, Pixar was a sensation, and the animated hits just kept coming: *A Bug's Life* in 1998, *Toy Story 2* in 1999, *Monsters, Inc.* in 2001, *Finding Nemo* in 2003, *The Incredibles* in 2004, *Cars* in 2006, *Ratatouille* in 2007, *WALL-E* in 2008, *Up* in 2009, *Toy Story 3* in 2010, and *Cars 2* in 2011.

In January 2006, Disney struck a deal to buy its partner Pixar in an all-stock transaction worth $7.4 billion. Jobs became the largest single shareholder in the Walt Disney Company as a result of this deal, with ownership of approximately 7 percent of the company's stock. Jobs's Disney holdings would exceed even those of former CEO Michael Eisner, who owned about 1.7 percent, and Disney family member Roy E. Disney, who held about 1 percent at the time the Pixar deal was struck. Jobs also gained a seat on the Disney board of directors.

Back at Apple, Jobs steadily brought the company back to the fore, with aggressive marketing and—most important, of course—jaw-dropping, innovative digital products.

Consider the iPod. It revolutionized the way people listen to music, not only serving as the dominant portable music player (sayonara, Sony Walkman) but also making digital music accessible just about anywhere through the iTunes store. Apple's development of the iPod was part of a broader plan for the company to branch into music distribution as well as consumer electronics.

When Apple released the iPhone in 2007, there was a similar plan in place. Apple burst into another key industry of the modern world, mobile communications. The multi-touch-display cell phone that facilitated this development builds on the features of the iPod and has ultimately revolutionized the mobile browsing scene. It's not for nothing that they call them "smart" phones.

And then came the iPad and iPad 2. We'll have to see what Apple comes up with next. All of Apple's growth and success have not been without controversy, however. Jobs insisted that product users and software developers play his way or hit the highway. Jobs didn't believe in open systems, allowing free, unfettered access to products and services—the way Google, Microsoft, and many others manage their e-worlds. Instead, Apple and Jobs wanted to make a buck whenever and wherever they could. Magazine and newspaper publishers, for example, have been disappointed at best and angry at worst over the iPad's rules for content and subscription purchases. Apple has censored some apps and has insisted on a 30 percent commission for any subscriptions sold. Said Forrester Research analyst James McQuivey in a BBC interview, "Apple envisions a world in which people don't consume any kind of digital media without its help." [79]

---

79 Patrick May, "Apple Makes Bid to Become Gatekeeper for Newspapers and Magazines," mediaIdeas, April 3, 2011, http://blog.mediaideas.net/2011/04/04/apple-makes-bid-to-become-gatekeeper-for-newspapers-and-magazines/.

138

Not everyone shares that vision. Apple is involved in a host of lawsuits, as both a plaintiff and a defendant, ranging from disputes over patents to antitrust allegations. Apple and Jobs have also taken heat for their outsourcing of many iPhone and iPod assembly jobs overseas, particularly to a Foxconn plant in Shenzhen, China, where harsh working conditions and low pay have led to a rash of worker suicides.

But the man and his company always seemed to weather every storm that came their way. Steve Jobs was aggressive, persuasive, effective, and fearless. An egomaniac too? You bet. Just take a look at his black-turtleneck performances. But he was a visionary. And it's safe to say our lives would be quite different without him and his company.

What is it about Apple products that makes them resonate so well with users throughout the world? Why can't we put them down? Why do we so enjoy working and playing with them? In other words, what is so special about Apple products' design?

First, simplicity. No clutter, no confusion. The designs never try to do too much at once or show too much in too little space. Then there's the attention to detail. Whether it's icons on a screen or logos on a carrying case, Apple does sweat the small stuff. Furthermore, the designs are consistent. Apple screens in every one of its products have the same look and feel and the same basic grid, in which navigation is intuitive. Finally, Apple products possess a quality that is hard to measure but apparent nonetheless: class. The designs are not sterile, not industrial, and not techie, but classy. You feel good about holding Apple products in your hands, putting them up to your ear, or opening them up on the tray table in front of you.

But most important is what the man himself, Steve Jobs, said about it: "Design is not just what it looks like and feels like. Design is how it works."[80]

For all his amazing intelligence, his business acumen, and his relentless aggressiveness, Jobs always was fearless and crazy enough to give design its due—to make sure his company's products worked well and looked good. That's the only way he'd have it. It was by design.

And now that Apple aggressiveness, that dedication to quality and design, will have to go on without the man himself. In yet another surprise announcement, Jobs, 56, revealed in late August 2011 that he was stepping down as the company's chief executive. Clearly his health dictated the decision. "I have always said that if there ever came a day when I could no longer meet my duties and expectations as Apple's CEO, I would be the first to let you know," Jobs wrote in a letter released by the company. "Unfortunately, that day has come."[81]

Just weeks later, on Oct. 5th, 2011, Job's ultimate day came. He died peacefully, with his family at his side. He's gone, but his company and its legacy live on. It's Apple, after all. Solid, creative, and well-designed.

---

80 Rob Walker, "The Guts of a New Machine," *New York Times*, November 30, 2003, http://www.nytimes.com/2003/11/30/magazine/30IPOD.html?ex=1386133200&en=750c9021e58923d5&ei=5007&partner=USERLAND.

81 David Streitfeld, "Job Steps Down at Apple, Saying He Can't Meet Duties," *New York Times*, August 24, 2011, http://www.nytimes.com/2011/08/25/technology/jobs-stepping-down-as-chief-of-apple.html?_r=1&hp.

140 Brick and Mortar

Design is what he does, what he lives for. He's one of the greatest architects the world has ever known. The projects he has worked on form an amazing list that would fill many pages of this book. Among them are L'Enfant Plaza Hotel in Washington, D.C., the Green Building at MIT, the National Center for Atmospheric Research in Colorado, the John F. Kennedy Library in Boston, Dallas City Hall, the East Building of the National Gallery of Art in Washington, D.C., the Fragrant Hill Hotel in China, the Bank of China building in Hong Kong, the glass and steel pyramid for the Louvre museum in Paris, the Morton H. Meyerson Symphony Center in Dallas, the Rock and Roll Hall of Fame in Cleveland, the Miho Museum in Japan, and the Museum of Islamic Art in Qatar. And that's just *some* of the buildings.

Also, he has received virtually every prize, award, and honor the architecture profession can bestow, including the AIA Gold Medal, Praemium Imperiale for Architecture, the Lifetime Achievement Award from the Cooper-Hewitt National Design Museum, and the Pritzker Prize, often called architecture's Nobel Prize.

I. M. Pei is in his nineties now and not slowing down. The spark, talent, and creative eye are still there, just like they were all those decades ago when the 18-year-old made a fearless and crazy decision to leave his native China for America. Why the life change? Because he liked Bing Crosby movies.

Pei knew he wanted to attend a first-rate architecture school in the United States—that was his serious, career-minded side. But he was fascinated by what he had seen of college life in Bing Crosby's early 1930s movies. Hollywood made 141 higher education seem like an amazing adventure.

"College life in the U.S. seemed to me to be mostly fun and games," he remembered decades later. "Since I was too young to be serious, I wanted to be part of it. You could get a feeling for it in Bing Crosby's movies. College life in America seemed very exciting to me. It's not real, we know that. Nevertheless, at that time it was very attractive to me. I decided that was the country for me."[82]

So Pei made his way by ship and train to Philadelphia to attend the University of Pennsylvania. But he was soon disappointed—in the academic offerings, not the social life. The school's architecture professors seemed stuck in the classic traditions of the Greeks and Romans. Pei had his sights on modern architecture—something new, something different. He transferred to the Massachusetts Institute of Technology.

But at MIT, the architecture school was more of the same, teaching and promoting the Beaux-Arts style with its emphasis on the classical. Pei stuck it out and did well academically, even though he was intrigued by the designs of the new International style and the Prairie School designs of Frank Lloyd Wright. He received his bachelor's of architecture degree in 1940 and planned to return to China to begin his design career. But the Japanese had invaded his homeland, and he stayed in America.

He soon met Eileen Loo, the woman whom he would

82 Gero von Boehm, *Conversations with I. M. Pei: Light is the Key* (New York: Prestel, 2000), 34.

marry and with whom he would raise a family and share a life. Loo enrolled in the landscape architecture program at Harvard University; Pei joined Harvard's Graduate School of Design. It was here that Pei worked with and got to know famed architects Walter Gropius and Marcel Breuer, both of whom were proponents of modern architecture. Pei's career took off like a rocket.

He received his master's from Harvard in 1946 and taught there for the next two years. He then went to work for New York real estate developer Webb and Knapp, designing apartment buildings, housing towers, a corporate building for Gulf Oil in Atlanta, the Roosevelt Field Shopping Mall, the Mile High Center in Denver, and Denver's Court House Square.

In 1955, he started his own firm, I. M. Pei and Associates, but continued to work with Webb and Knapp. Among the projects Pei and his firm designed over the next 35 years are Kips Bay Towers in Manhattan, Society Hill Towers in Pennsylvania, and the National Center for Atmospheric Research (NCAR) complex, mentioned previously. Pei considered the NCAR project his breakout design; it won him notoriety and praise.

The NCAR was followed by the S. I. Newhouse School of Public Communications at Syracuse University and the John F. Kennedy Presidential Library and Museum, his signature creation. Jacqueline Kennedy herself chose Pei for the job for both professional and personal reasons. She liked that Pei didn't fit any particular mold; he used techniques and ideas from just about anyone or anywhere. "He didn't seem to have just one way to solve a problem," said

Mrs. Kennedy. "He seemed to approach each commission thinking only of it and then develop a way of making something beautiful."[83]

She also felt a special connection with Pei; he reminded her in many ways of her late husband. "Pei was so full of promise, like Jack," she said. "They were born in the same year. I decided to take a great leap with him."[84]

The Kennedy project was incredibly challenging for Pei, with stops and starts and rethinking and reimagining along the way. It was dedicated in October 1979. Pei calls it the most important commission of his life.

The projects continued and haven't stopped yet. The entire world is his drawing board for more grand designs, traditional structures, and breathtaking advances. Jacqueline Kennedy had it right when she said he didn't have just one way to solve a problem. I. M. Pei's style cannot be described by any one adjective. He doesn't like the idea of architectural trends and "schools." There is no Pei School. To him, everything is fair game. "An individual building, the style in which it is going to be designed and built, is not that important," he said. "The important thing, really, is the community. How does it affect life?" And later he said, "I believe that architecture is a pragmatic art. To become art it must be built on a foundation of necessity."[85]

---

83 Carter Wiseman, *I. M. Pei: A Profile in American Architecture* (New York: H.N. Abrams, 2001), 98.

84 Ibid., 99.

85 Barbaralee Diamonstein, *American Architecture Now* (New York: Rizzoli, 1980), 145.

The citation for Pei's 1983 Pritzker Prize sums up the man
144 and his work best: "Ieoh Ming Pei has given this century some
of its most beautiful interior spaces and exterior forms. . . .
His versatility and skill in the use of materials approach the
level of poetry."[86]
And perhaps we have an affable crooner to thank for it all.
If the fearless and crazy I. M. Pei hadn't been so intrigued
by Bing Crosby and the college life he promised, the young
student may have never gotten on that boat and sailed off to
America and into architectural history.

Multidimensional Man

His mother was a painter, and his father was an engineer.
So it's not that surprising that this Ontario-born-and-bred
risk taker is a remarkable scientist/artist combination. In fact,
to create the greatest work of his amazing career, the artist
in him had to wait several years for the science—his and
others'—to catch up and make his vision a reality.

This dual-purpose genius is none other than James Cameron, the most successful filmmaker in Hollywood history.
And the story that had to wait for the technology before it
could become digital reality is, of course, Cameron's *Avatar*,
the biggest box-office smash ever.

As a young man, Cameron assumed his natural bent, and
the tech side of the filmmaking business was where it landed.

---

86 "I. M. Pei, 1983 Laureate: Jury Citation," Pritzker Architecture Prize, http://
www.pritzkerprize.com/laureates/1983/jury.html.

He drove a truck on weekdays but hunkered down in a University of Southern California library on weekends, photocopying 145 scholarly works and dissertations about optical printing and film stocks. "This is not bull," he said later in an interview with *Popular Mechanics*. "I gave myself a great course on film FX for the cost of the copying."[87]

His first gig in the biz was with legendary low-budget producer/director Roger Corman as part of the effects crew on the forgettable 1980 flick *Battle Beyond the Stars*. Then it was on to meatier fare such as 1981's *Piranha II: The Spawning*, which Cameron wrote and directed. Then came the hits in rapid succession: *The Terminator* (1984), *Aliens* (1986), *The Abyss* (1989), *Terminator 2: Judgment Day* (1991), *True Lies* (1994), *Titanic* (1997), and *Dark Angel* (2000–2002). *Titanic*, of course, was like nothing before. It earned 11 Academy Awards, including Best Picture and Best Director, for Cameron. It was the highest-grossing movie ever, at $1.8 billion. But as we all know, there's a new box-office champ: Cameron's 2009 megahit, *Avatar*, at $2.7 billion.

The movies reflect their creator. They are the art-science combination that is at the core of the man himself. More often than not, Cameron writes the screenplays. Among his screenwriting credits are *The Terminator*, *Aliens*, *The Abyss*, *Titanic*, and of course, *Avatar*.

On the tech side, *The Abyss* featured ahead-of-the-curve underwater lighting effects, developed by Hollywood inventor

---

87 Anne Thompson, "How James Cameron's Innovative New 3D Tech Created *Avatar*," *Popular Mechanics*, January 1, 2010, http://www.popularmechanics.com/technology/digital/visual-effects/4339455.

Vince Pace. And it was that kind of cutting-edge design—
primarily on the video-optical side—that captured Cameron's imagination and got his creative juices flowing. He helped found the special effects company Digital Domain in the early 1990s. Those underwater effects for *The Abyss* were the basis for his amazing "liquid metal" effect in 1991's *Terminator 2: Judgment Day*. Cameron and Pace designed a unique high-definition 3-D camera for Cameron's 2003 documentary, *Ghosts of the Abyss*, which explored the wreck of the *Titanic*.

Every Cameron project tests the limits of what is possible in the science of moviemaking. If it hasn't been invented yet, he designs it himself and tries it out. Bruce Davis, former executive director of the Academy of Motion Picture Arts and Sciences, admires Cameron's "willingness to incorporate new technologies in his films without waiting for them to be perfected. They call this 'building the parachute on the way down.'"[88]

They also call it fearless and crazy.

But Cameron did have to wait for science to catch up before he could shoot *Avatar*. In 1995, he wrote an 80-page treatment of the story, with working title *Project 880*. It wasn't until 10 years later that the 3-D technology was ready for him to move forward. But even then, it was slow going, with the film's May 2009 release pushed back to December (which, incidentally, gave 3,000 additional theaters more time to install the expensive 3-D projectors).

Avatar is composed almost entirely of computer-generated animation. Cameron used a modified version of the Fusion

---

88 Ibid.

camera for the live-action sequences. The new 3-D camera creates an augmented-reality view for Cameron as he shoots, 147 sensing its position on a motion-capture stage and then integrating the live actors into computer-generated environments on the viewfinder. Confused? Me too. The point is that Cameron's specially designed equipment and painstaking technique make the 3-D picture immersive; it swallows you up to bring you deep into the exotic world of Pandora.

Cameron's *Avatar* tale and the amazing way he brought it to the screen were clearly worth the wait. The man who can design a story and put it on the page and then design a camera to bring that story to life is the most daring risk taker in Hollywood.

Coming attractions? Here's the lineup:

- → 2013: *Fantastic Voyage* (executive producer)
- → 2014: *Avatar 2* (director, writer, producer, editor)
- → 2015: *Avatar 3* (director, writer, producer, editor)

You'd better get your 3-D glasses ready. On second thought, hold off on those glasses. They're likely to be obsolete because there's no telling what James Cameron, the amazing artist-scientist of Hollywood, will have come up with by then.

■　■　■

→ MY TAKE

One of my favorite definitions of design comes from Sir George Cox, writing in his *Cox Review*: "Design is what links creativity and innovation. It shapes ideas to become practical and attractive propositions for users or customers. Design may be described as creativity deployed to a specific end."[89]

Another fitting definition says that "design is all around you; everything man-made has been designed, whether consciously or not."[90]

There has never *not* been design; design is involved in everything from the earliest drawings on a cave wall to the latest smart phone app. It's the aesthetic—the look and feel of something. But more important, it's the practicality and the functionality. Design looks at how things work, how they do their jobs, and how they could do their jobs better.

There's a simple way to tell if your neighborhood park has been well designed. As you walk around and through it, notice whether there are paths worn into the grass where your neighbors have left the designated, constructed sidewalk or trail and made their way by a different route, often shorter and sometimes more scenic. In your park, people "vote" with their feet. They decide which route is best. If people have to forge their own trails, the designers got it wrong.

It's that way in business too. You can get a headache thinking of all the product flops over the years—even Apple has had a few (remember the Apple Newton MessagePad?).

89 Sir George Cox, *Cox Review of Creativity in Business: Building on the UK's Strengths* (London: Her Majesty's Treasury, 2005).

90 See Mat Hunter, "What Design Is and Why It Matters," Design Council, http://www.designcouncil.org.uk/about-design/What-design-is-and-why-it-matters/.

Quite often those flops were because the design was wrong, impractical, or too confusing—design run amok, as I like to say.

Design takes ideas—the intangibles, the abstract—and makes them concrete, usable, applicable, and appropriate. Design solves problems. If it doesn't, the product is soon abandoned and forgotten.

Sometimes a designer gets a little too artsy and forgets that practical part. If you want to witness an example of that, just show up on a construction project site and ask the contractors what they think of the architect's design details. You're likely to get an earful.

Because design is so important, it's seldom "discovered" in a vacuum, seldom come upon by some lonely nerd in a eureka moment. Instead, design is a collaborative process. It requires brainstorming and teamwork. It means hit and miss, trial and error. That's why I love it. In my new business, making movies, collaboration is essential. Without it there is nothing, and certainly not a movie.

Steve Jobs had hundreds if not thousands of product designers at Apple. I. M. Pei has his design team and all the contractors that work with him. James Cameron hires the best and brightest technology talent in Hollywood. And for those three and you, design happens from the beginning of your life-wealth plan. It starts with your vision and goals; affects every component of your plans to make those visions and goals realities; and is always there when you execute your plans, when you network and market, and when you react to the unknowns. Design is like the spine of your life-wealth plan. In fact, creating (and living) a life-wealth plan is in itself an exercise in design.

150

So how do you go about designing? Is there a method? A process? Later in this book, I give you some simple exercises to help you get started designing your life-wealth plan. In the meantime, here are several ways to approach more general design challenges, as practiced by those who get paid to do so:

- Use the KISS principle (keep it simple, stupid). Eliminate the unnecessary.
- There is more than one way to do it (TIMTOWTDI). Allow for many ways of doing the same thing.
- Incorporate use-centered design, in which the primary emphasis is on how the item will be *used*.
- Think about user-centered design. Most important are the needs, wants, and limitations of the end *user* of the item.
- Consider critical design—design that makes a statement or offers a critique of the values and practices in a culture.[91]

Look at those approaches again, thinking of Jobs, Pei, and Cameron. Their works have these methods written all over them.

But let's not get too academic. You know good design when you see it, and more important, you know good design

---

91 "Approaches to Design," Wikipedia, March 21, 2011, http://en.wikipedia. org/wiki/Design.

when you use it. As Procter & Gamble CEO A. G. Lafley says, "Your products run for election every day, and good design is critical to winning the campaign."[92]

People—consumers, clients, investors—vote for good design, with their feet and hands, with their brains and hearts. As noted design writer Brenda Laurel says, "A design isn't finished until someone is using it."[93]

---

92 Jennifer Reingold, "What P&G Knows About the Power of Design," *Fast Company*, June 1, 2005, http://www.fastcompany.com/magazine/95/design-qa.html.

93 Sander Baumann, "Beautiful and Inspiring Designers Quotes," designworkplan.com, December 8, 2008, http://www.designworkplan.com/design/inspiring-quotes.htm.

8

SWING AND A MISS

The men who try to do something and fail are infinitely better than those who try to do nothing and succeed.

—LLOYD JONES

If it were easy, the word *risk* would not apply. Being fearless and crazy by definition means things often go astray. They don't pan out. You fall flat on your face. It's an unmitigated disaster. A bomb, a bust. What were you thinking? Are you crazy?

In your personal and professional life, as an embracer of the fearless and crazy, you will fail. You will want to quit. You'll say never again. Because it's risky—but because it's risky, it has its rewards. If not this time, maybe next time.

The following stories describe a few notable fearless and

crazy decisions that backfired. I present them simply as a
reminder that if it were easy, everybody would be doing it.

Gull Doors

Nobody had ever seen anything like it. The first DeLorean
DMC-12 rolled off the line at its Dunmurry, Northern Ire-
land, assembly plant in early 1981. Its body panels were
made of stainless steel, and most amazing of all, it featured
gull-wing doors, which opened up and out, giving it the look
of a bird taking flight or preparing to land. It was a fearless and crazy creation, the brainchild of John DeLorean, a
former General Motors executive.

Perhaps the unusual new vehicle was too crazy. Sales
were tepid, engineering delays were frequent, and cost over-
runs were eating up any money that did come in. DeLorean placed his hopes on a pending stock issue in the United
States, which would raise as much as $27 million, but the
Securities and Exchange Commission had too many questions about the company's viability and canceled the IPO. In
two years of production, just 9,000 cars were made.

DeLorean's personal problems didn't help matters. In
October 1982, he was arrested in an FBI sting operation and
charged with conspiring to smuggle $24 million worth of
cocaine into the United States. Although he was acquitted,
his reputation was in ruins. DeLorean Motor Company
declared bankruptcy.

But the story wasn't quite over. In the mid-1980s, the *Back
to the Future* movie trilogy made the DeLorean something

of a cultural icon. Says the first film's Marty McFly, "Wait a minute, Doc. Ah . . . are you telling me you built a time 155 machine out of a DeLorean?"

Answers "Doc," Dr. Emmett Brown, "The way I see it, if you're going to build a car into a time machine, why not do it with some style?"

Style, indeed. Fearless and crazy. But gone.

Circumnavigator

She would follow a close-to-the-equator route—29,000 miles in all—thus besting Wiley Post's northern midlatitude route. Post was a legend in aviation circles by 1937, only two years after he and comedian/commentator Will Rogers were killed in a tragic crash in Alaska. But Amelia Earhart had always tried to do better—especially better than the men. Her accomplishments in the air and on the ground had made her one of the most famous people in the world, male or female.

She was the first aviatrix to fly solo across the Atlantic. She was the first person to fly the Atlantic twice. She was the first woman to receive the Distinguished Flying Cross. She was the first woman to fly nonstop, coast-to-coast across the United States. She was the first person to fly solo between Honolulu, Hawaii, and Oakland, California. Her list of firsts and records goes on and on.

She also was an author of two best-selling books about her flying adventures, and she helped found the Ninety-nines, an organization of female pilots. She was a visiting faculty member of Purdue University's aviation department. She was a member of the National Woman's Party and a supporter of the Equal Rights Amendment.

But now it was time to circumnavigate the globe—like no one else before her.

The plan was to go west, starting from Oakland. But when she and navigators Fred Noonan and Harry Manning, along with technical advisor Paul Mantz, got to Honolulu, their Lockheed Electra 10E had a series of technical problems and damages that ended the attempt. When repairs were complete, Earhart's supporters financed a quiet flight back to the mainland and eventually to Miami, Florida. This would be the embarkation point for the second attempt, still along an equatorial route but this time heading east. And this time with only Earhart and Noonan in the cockpit.

They departed on June 1, 1937, with numerous stops along the way in South America, Africa, the Indian subcontinent, and Southeast Asia. They landed in Lae, New Guinea, on June 29. They had flown approximately 22,000 of the 29,000 total miles. From Lae, they planned to fly to remote Howland Island, then to Honolulu and on to California, and then cross-country to their origin in Miami.

The tragic result is the stuff of legends, tall tales, and conspiracy theories: the world will likely never know why or how, but Earhart, Noonan, and their Lockheed Electra disappeared on July 2, 1937, somewhere near Howland, despite a series of maddening, confusing radio transmissions to the escort ship waiting at the island to guide them in.

Amelia Earhart and her doomed final flight have become a pop culture mainstay, most recently by way of a 2009 feature film starring Hilary Swank as Earhart and breathless news reports in late 2010 that bones found on a deserted South Pacific island could be hers. But the mystery remains unsolved, and it's too good a story to ever go away. She took a chance; she paid the price.

"Please know that I am aware of the hazards," she said when people wondered why she did what she did. "I want to do it because I want to do it. Women must try to do things as men have tried. When they fail, their failure must be a challenge to others."[94]

Merging Traffic

It seemed like a good deal at the time. In fact, the press called it the most significant, game-changing corporate merger in history, a "transformative" moment, the beginning of a new media era. Photos taken the day of the deal's announcement, January 10, 2000, show the companies' two leaders beaming with smiles, their hands clasped above their heads like champion boxers celebrating a knockout.

A knockout it was. Today the merger of AOL and Time Warner is considered the worst corporate transaction in history, the granddaddy of all business school case studies. The value of the deal was a stunning $350 billion, still the largest in U.S. business history. It was fearless; it was crazy. And its failure was monumental.

---

94 "Biography," Amelia Earhart: The Official Website, http://www.ameliaearhart.com/about/bio2.html.

It was all about the Internet. Online communication seemed poised to change every traditional, mainstream media business model. AOL's stock price was flying high, about twice that of Time Warner's. Gushed Time Warner CEO Gerald Levin about the Internet: "It had begun to create unprecedented and instantaneous access to every form of media and to unleash immense possibilities for economic growth, human understanding, and creative expression."[95]

Wow. AOL cofounder Steve Case was a little less philosophical but equally impressed with what the two companies had wrought: "This is a historic moment in which new media has truly come of age."[96]

But stuff happened on the road to Internet nirvana. From the start, the "merger" was a little odd. It was billed as a marriage of equals, but AOL, with its more valuable stock, was actually acquiring Time Warner. AOL would own 55 percent of the new company; Time Warner, 45 percent. The new board's seats would be divided equally, however. Levin would be CEO; Case would be chairman.

Federal Trade Commission approval took a year and was granted despite the objections of FTC economists who said the deal didn't make financial sense. By May of 2000, the dot-com bubble had begun to burst; online advertising had

---

95 Tim Arango, "How the AOL-Time Warner Merger Went So Wrong," *New York Times*, January 10, 2010, http://www.nytimes.com/2010/01/11/business/media/11merger.html?pagewanted=all.

96 Ibid.

slowed; and AOL's financial forecasts, on which the deal was based, looked dubious. Most important, the world was 159 moving quickly toward high-speed Internet access and abandoning AOL's ubiquitous dial-up service.

On top of all that, the two companies' cultures were decidedly different. Their respective executives seemed to be at war, blaming each other for all the negativity. Secret documents leaked by Time Warner execs revealed that AOL had been inflating its revenues. The SEC and the Department of Justice both launched investigations. The company paid large fines and had to go back and restate earnings. Steve Case stepped down as chairman. Many employees and investors lost significant money, including Ted Turner, who lost $8 billion—80 percent of his worth at the time.[97]

The marriage was over. Today the two companies are single again, and their combined worth is only about 15 percent of their worth on the day of the merger.

Blockbuster deals are sometimes too fearless and crazy for their own good.

Interestingly, in February 2011, AOL announced it would acquire The Huffington Post, the influential news and comment site founded and run by Arianna Huffington. She will be in charge. Execs from both companies are gushing about the perfect fit and the powerful synergies.

Déjà vu?

---

97 Ibid.

160 Changing the Formula

If it ain't broke, don't fix it. It wasn't, but they did. And they paid dearly.

It was the numbers that made them do it. Coke, the Coca-Cola Company's flagship beverage, had been the dominant market leader for decades. In fact, just after World War II, its market share was 60 percent. But by the early 1980s, Pepsi-Cola, Coke's archrival, was making phenomenal gains with aggressive marketing, including its television "Taste Test" commercials. Coke's market share had shrunk to 24 percent. Something had to be done.

Coca-Cola senior executives commissioned a secret initiative called "Project Kansas" to test and perfect a new flavor for Coke. The secret tests were encouraging. The new formula gave Coke a sweeter taste, closer to that of Pepsi. And the new formula beat out both traditional Coke and Pepsi in focus groups. But a significant minority of those tasters—about 10 to 12 percent—was adamantly against any change, and they made their feelings known. Coke execs didn't realize it at the time, but this sort of reaction was a harbinger of things to come.

Management decided to move forward. Coke would be replaced by the newly formulated Coke and, in fact, called New Coke. They would introduce it with a marketing and media blitz that would be like no other and send Pepsi back to whatever bottling plant it came from. The New Coke announcement and debut was scheduled for April 23, 1985, but Pepsi officials got wind of it and took out ads in the few days before April 23, claiming they'd won the "cola wars."

The big day came, and Coca-Cola held a press conference at New York's Lincoln Center. Coca-Cola CEO Robert Goizueta did the honors, but his performance was less than scintillating. The press had been fed tough questions about the change from Pepsi officials, most of them versions of the basic "Why?" Goizueta stumbled over his words as he described New Coke's taste as "smoother, uh, uh, rounder yet, uh, bolder . . . a more harmonious flavor."[98] You'd think he might have rehearsed a little.

But despite the shaky beginning, New Coke seemed to be a hit. Coca-Cola stock went up immediately, and virtually everyone in the country knew about the switch, especially after a series of major marketing events. Coke sales jumped 8 percent over the year before.

But not every Coke drinker was happy. Southerners especially complained about the new taste. Coke had always been their drink, and they felt this change showed a lack of respect for their region. Journalists, comedians, and talk show hosts across the country got on the negative bandwagon. When ads for New Coke flashed on the scoreboard at the Houston Astrodome, fans booed. Fidel Castro, a Coke drinker, called New Coke yet another sign of American capitalist decadence. There were public protests, with people emptying New Coke

---

98 Mark Pendergrast, *For God, Country and Coca-Cola: The Definitive History of the Great American Soft Drink and the Company That Makes It* (New York: Basic Books, 2000), 352.

cans into the gutter. Even Coca-Cola bottling companies were grumbling. Pepsi loved all the wailing and gnashing of teeth and reworked its ads to take advantage of Coke's backlash storm.

Bashing the New Coke had become the "in" thing to do; it was chic. Even if New Coke had been the nectar of the gods, it was probably too late to save it. On July 10, 1985, just 77 days after New Coke's introduction, Coca-Cola executives announced the return to the original formula. "Old" Coke was back, with the name Coca-Cola Classic or simply Coke Classic. ABC's Peter Jennings interrupted *General Hospital* to share the news with viewers. On the floor of the U.S. Senate, Senator David Pryor called the reintroduction "a meaningful moment in U.S. history."[99] The public had prevailed. A giant corporation had listened to the masses.

A fearless and crazy corporate decision had backfired. Spectacularly.

Or did it? Coke Classic sales grew by leaps and bounds. Coca-Cola's market dominance became stronger than ever. Cola drinkers applauded the company for listening and bought its products with fervor and loyalty like never before. In fact, Coca-Cola rebounded so well with its Coke Classic that some cynics think the whole thing might have been a giant marketing ploy, a PR trick to win back customers. Now, *that* would be fearless and crazy.

■ ■ ■

---

99 Ibid., 364.

⇒ MY TAKE

Our four subjects discussed here made fearless and crazy decisions and lost. That will happen a lot, of course. They don't call it *risk* for nothing. Amelia Earhart paid the ultimate price for her decision. Time Warner and DeLorean never fully recovered from theirs. As for Coke, it bounced back beautifully from its miss and is as strong as ever.

So why do some swings lead to home runs and others nothing but air? In the world of corporations and entrepreneurs, why do some businesses fail while others flourish? In terms of our ongoing discussion of life-wealth planning, why are some people and companies able to deal with the unknowns and others aren't?

There are the obvious, most common reasons, of course: too little money, a product or service nobody wants, strong competition, and so on. Business writer Will Limkemann lists and analyzes a few more that are often overlooked. Briefly, they are:

- ⇒ **Employee theft,** including embezzlement, cash theft, inventory or equipment theft, and even intellectual property theft. Examples include the bartender who gives his pals an occasional free drink and the office employee who takes home Post-it Notes and printer paper.

- ⇒ **Unplanned growth.** If a business is so successful that it can't keep up with the demand, every shred of goodwill and good PR it has earned could be squandered. For example, a new restaurant opens to amazingly positive buzz but can't handle the resulting rush. Service is terrible; the food takes forever. And no one comes back.

➡ **IT failures.** There isn't a business in America that doesn't rely on some form of Internet, email, social media, or app. If your website goes dark, even for just a short time, you can be in trouble. Consumers and clients expect—and demand—online access, service, and information.

➡ **Poor record keeping.** Limkemann cites an amazing statistic from a survey of businesses that filed for bankruptcy: 58 percent of those failed businesses did little or no record keeping. If you hate keeping track of things or aren't any good at it, hire someone to do it. There's more to business than handshakes and lunches.

➡ **Failure to seek and use advice.** Nobody does it alone. We stand on the shoulders of others. Find a friend or colleague who has been there and done that. Contact the professional, governmental, and service agencies dedicated to helping. Take a class. Read a book (even this one). There's no excuse for being deliberately ignorant.[100]

So these are things to watch out for, obstacles to avoid. But what do you proactively do to advance your professional career and minimize the chances of failure? How can

---

100 Will Limkemann, "Five Surprising Reasons for Business Failure and How to Prevent Them," *Ezine Articles*, June 25, 2009, http://ezinearticles. com/?Five-Surprising-Reasons-For-Business-Failure-And-How-to-Prevent-Them&id=2501260.

you avoid the misses while still being unafraid to make the fearless and crazy swings? Minimizing the risk of failure, personally or professionally, is possible if you focus on one simple, all-important word: knowledge. Socrates—another risk taker who paid the ultimate price—said it best: "Know thyself."

A key step in business development and planning is knowing your competition and, more important, knowing yourself and what you are capable of. When I say "you" and "yourself," I mean you as an entrepreneur and your company.

So how do you get to know yourself and your competition? Go to the library? Surf the web? Ask around? Go through your competitor's trash? Well, all of that might help. But there is a popular business analytical tool that can provide some assistance. It's popular because it's effective. It's called SWOT analysis. It's a strategic method you can use to get to know yourself and your company so you can better decide a course of action, more successfully launch a new product, or more effectively take on a new initiative. You can use the SWOT tool to pause for a bit, to catch your breath, just before your fearless and crazy marketing of Product You and the company you are begins.

As mentioned in Chapter 1, SWOT analysis is a key tool in the marketing component of life-wealth. In fact, a SWOT analysis is an excellent first marketing step. You may have heard of SWOT analysis and may have even used it. If so, this refresher should make you feel even more confident.

Basically, SWOT analysis involves examining and evaluating strengths, weaknesses, opportunities, and threats (hence the acronym). In business, these categories are defined as

follows:

- **Strengths:** *internal* characteristics of the business or team that give it an advantage over others in the industry. *Internal* simply means specific to you and your situation (or to that of the business you're analyzing).

- **Weaknesses:** *internal* characteristics that place the firm at a disadvantage relative to others.

- **Opportunities:** *external* chances to make greater sales or profits in the current environment at the current time. *External* simply means outside the business—out in the community or marketplace.

- **Threats:** *external* elements in the environment that could cause trouble for the business.

SWOT analysis is key for me in all my business planning and strategizing—everything from deciding whether to enter into a joint venture to expanding one of my companies, from discontinuing a product or service to making key personnel decisions. Sometimes I write down the lists and create the SWOT grid; other times I use SWOT analysis instinctively in my head on the fly.

Let's focus on a SWOT analysis of a businessperson, an entrepreneur—you. To begin, you must understand that you are at the center of whatever business you're running and have various products and services to offer. Similarly, big corporations have their various departments, branches, and offices, plus all the people that work in those departments, branches, and offices. The corporations have cost centers and profit centers. So do you. Think of yourself objectively, as a product. Product You could be anything you are good at; it could be freelance photography, web design, running a nursery, coaching executives, or making sports drinks. You are the hub of the wheel and all your various companies, skills, products, or services, the spokes that come out from that central brand—you.

Let's look at an example I'm intimately familiar with: Product Arthur Wylie. Arthur Wylie's products and services ("spokes") include:

- Motivational speaking
- Financial consulting services
- Online consulting business
- Real estate services
- Multilevel marketing
- Feature film development

If we don't think of ourselves as products suitable for analysis—if we think of ourselves as simple nine-to-five drones, working for the man—there isn't much of a wheel, no "spokes" to list. They pay you; you go home and hope the job is there tomorrow. It's all about them, not you. They are the product, not you. Do you see the difference? When you become a product—when you analyze your strengths, weaknesses, opportunities, and threats to determine your ultimate success—you are in control of your own destiny.

That analysis can be as lofty as a personal assessment of your character and personality and your place in the world, or it can be a nitty-gritty assessment of a business opportunity. The SWOT tool is so simple yet so valuable.

Let's look at a business opportunity. We'll create a simple case study and run it through the SWOT paces.

Daniel has opened a used bookstore featuring nothing but histories and biographies. No cookbooks, *Dummies* guides, or vampire tales. His store is located in a restored building in a gentrified part of town adjacent to the university. He calls his bookstore Past Lives.

- ➡ **Strengths:** With a location so near the world of professors and students, he has a ready-made clientele for his products. There will be plenty of books to buy, sell, and trade and lots of foot traffic in the area. His vintage building also helps the marketing; the store's name is a plus as well.

- ➡ **Weaknesses:** That old building has ongoing maintenance problems. Furthermore, there's no room in the cramped store for couches, a coffee counter, or other perks. Also, Daniel must create and maintain a database of the books on his shelves—a database that must be updated constantly. And his clientele will expect a website—more work that will keep him from minding the store and interacting with customers.

- ➡ **Opportunities:** The store could host readings, receptions, and book signings with the talented university faculty, many of whom are biographers and historians. Low-cost student labor is available to help Daniel keep the shelves full and handle those computer tasks.

- ➡ **Threats:** Chain restaurants and retailers are changing the tone and tenor of the neighborhood. The campus bookstore buys and resells used books. The Kindle, Nook, and iPad revolution means there will be fewer customers for ink-on-paper products and fewer young people interested in browsing Daniel's shelves.

In SWOT analysis, you want to understand what makes you strong as a professional or as a business prospect and what your business challenges are. The driving question is: What makes you better than anyone else in that particular field, for that particular task, or for that particular position? Or what are the factors and conditions that are keeping you from being better than everyone else?

When I was new to the financial services game, my answer to the first question was that, unlike many of the financial planners at those big-office, big-name, big-money organizations, I was hungry for success, I was young and determined, I had passion and stamina, and what's more, I had a proven success story in myself. My SWOT analysis back then looked something like this:

Strengths

- ➡ The stock market was soaring.
- ➡ Because my investment company was a small, online

operation at the time, I was able to compete with the
"big boys" without many up-front expenses.

- ➡ I was young and going after young money. My target clients wanted young blood. I could easily relate to them. They were new doctors, college graduates, and middle-income workers—primarily new money that was typically overlooked.

- ➡ I was willing to grow my own assets slowly and steadily by growing my clients' assets, instead of continually going after the home run, the big deal.

- ➡ I created financial products that addressed my clients' specific needs according to their particular investment time lines (i.e., products for short-term, mid-term, or long-term goals).

- ➡ I was getting a steady stream of referrals because my business was small and consequently my services were personal, caring, and appropriate—something the big companies with all their assets and spreadsheets couldn't match.

Next, the weaknesses. What things do you need to work on? How can you overcome those weaknesses and be more competitive? In my case, I knew many considered my age a weakness, but I was determined to make it a strength. That's why I took so many extra classes, earned so many certifications, and managed on such a lean budget. The following are my weaknesses as an investment advisor. Notice that even though they are internal (unique to me), they ended up being external; they were perceptions by others, by the market. Yet that didn't mean I could trivialize them. After all, as discussed previously, perception is reality.

Weaknesses

➡ Age: This didn't really hold me back because, as mentioned above, I targeted clients who were also young and who shared many of the same financial goals. We spoke the same language. Had I been going after "old money," gray-haired retirees, my youth definitely would have been a weakness.

➡ Race: Certainly if I had been trying to get clients at an Aryan Nations rally, this would have been a weakness. But my race helped me attract clients who were people of color. Obviously, we had something in common immediately. We could relate.

➡ Lack of capital: A weakness, sure. So I dealt with it: I worked more jobs, got more credit, and found investors. I controlled my costs.

➡ Lack of experience: This was an initial weakness, but it didn't last long. I managed my own money well at a young age. I owned stocks, bonds, real estate, and many other assets, frequently trading those assets and growing my wealth. I also teamed up with a brokerage firm that had been in business for more than a hundred years to handle all my trades and compliance issues, giving me and my company an aura of stability and creditability.

Next, we look at opportunities. What are your opportunities? What is your next level of profitability, and what do you need to do to reach that next level? What other areas of personal and professional development do you need to achieve to accomplish your overall goals? Here's how my list of opportunities looked:

Opportunities

Diversifying into various income streams, including:

➡ Real estate
➡ Entertainment
➡ Public speaking
➡ Publishing
➡ Wealth management—institutional sales
➡ Bicoastal operations
➡ Online marketing

Last, we explore threats. What things could put you out of business if you aren't able to address them and eliminate them early on? What might prevent you from achieving your goals? As I was establishing and growing my business, these were my threats, both to my company and to me as a brand:

Threats

➡ Decline in the market
➡ Increased competition
➡ More online trading companies
➡ Increased regulation leading to increase in cost of doing business
➡ Employee turnover in an emerging organization

Doing the SWOT analysis helped me then, and it helps me now. It has become part of my standard operating proce- dure as an entrepreneur, as a brand. It's key to my marketing efforts. I don't leave home without it.

Time to SWOT analyze yourself, even if you've done it before in your career. Everything is changing; everything is in flux, always. If you need a little help getting your SWOT started, I provide step-by-step guidance in Chapter 10.

As you work on your SWOT analysis, either now or when you get to Chapter 10, make the four lists, even if you have only two or three items for each. Keep those lists handy for a few days or a week or so, because you'll think of more strengths, weaknesses, opportunities, and threats from time to time, and you'll want to add them on. Keep the lists on your nightstand; we all know how insights pop into our heads when we're staring up at the dark ceiling.

By doing all this, you're getting to know yourself better, and you'll be able to market yourself better. If you know yourself better, your odds for success increase significantly. You're training yourself for future fearless and crazy decisions. Because you know who you are, what you're doing, and what is possible, those fearless and crazy decisions will be hits, if not home runs. You won't often swing and miss.

9

PERSONAL PASSION

Chase down your passion like it's the last bus of the night.

—GLADE BYRON ADDAMS

Sometimes there's no other explanation than the most basic one of all: I just had to do it. No logic. No rationale. No pros and cons list. No SWOT analysis. No postmortem afterward. Instead, a personal, from-the-gut or from-the-heart decision that answered a calling, put out a fire, or fulfilled a dream. And it's the lucky ones among us who come to those forks in the road and have to make that decision to either follow their heart or listen to their head. It's emotion versus intellect. They either step off that cliff or they spend their lives wondering what could have happened.

176 CEO Coach

Joe Moglia earned his bachelor's degree from Fordham University and his master's from the University of Delaware. He spent seventeen years at Merrill Lynch, serving on the executive committees for both the institutional business and private client business. He was also responsible for all Merrill Lynch's investment products, its insurance company, its 401(k) business, and its middle-market business. He left Merrill Lynch in 2001 to become chief executive officer of online broker and financial services company Ameritrade, founded and based in Omaha, Nebraska. In his seven years at the helm, Ameritrade's client assets grew from $24 billion to more than $300 billion, while its market capitalization grew from $700 million to $12 billion. He engineered two significant Ameritrade acquisitions: Datek Online Holdings in 2002 and rival TD Waterhouse in 2006. The price tag on that second buy was $2.9 billion. The company's name became TD Ameritrade. In 2008, the year the world economy nose-dived, TD Ameritrade recorded its sixth straight year of record profits. Needless to say, its leader was doing something right. How's that for a résumé?

Then came that fearless and crazy moment. In March 2008, Joe Moglia, CEO of TD Ameritrade and one of the most respected, successful businessmen in the country, announced he would be walking away from his corner-office life in six short months. He would give up all the perks, all the prestige, and all the money to pursue his passion.

In September 2008, the first day of the rest of his life began. Moglia became an unpaid voluntary assistant coach and mentor for the University of Nebraska football team. His official title was executive advisor to the head football coach, Bo Pelini. Moglia worked 70 or more hours a week doing the mundane grunt work of a Division I football program, including studying playbooks, watching film, attending meetings and practices, and taking notes. He wasn't much more than a glorified intern.

But there was a bit more to it. Moglia's stellar corporate career and his charismatic personality made him an ideal mentor for both the coaches and the players. Said Pelini, "I knew Joe was a proven commodity, but after talking with him it was 'Why not bring him in, and get a different perspective?' He wanted to learn from me? Well, I wanted to learn from him."[101]

Moglia was no stranger to football, of course. As a young man, he had coached several high school teams and small colleges back east. He was defensive coordinator at Dartmouth from 1981 to 1983, when he decided to pursue a financial career and entered the Merrill Lynch training program. The rest would have been business history, except for that fearless and crazy decision in 2008.

Throughout those corporate glory years, the football flame burned brightly in Moglia's heart. When he took the Nebraska

---

101 Jon Wertheim, "Nebraska's Billion-Dollar Assistant," *Sports Illustrated*, September 30, 2010, http://sportsillustrated.cnn.com/2010/writers/jon_wertheim/09/28/nebraska.asst/index.html.

position, some of his friends and family members told him he was nuts: "At this point in your life, you're working seven days a week, living in a hotel? Grow up!" Others were supportive: "When you can do anything with your life and you're willing to sacrifice like this, it's passion! Go for it and follow your heart!"[102]

To Moglia, his life-changing decision wasn't all that crazy. "Honestly, to me it's not that strange," he said in an interview with *Sports Illustrated.* "I'm not some business guy who gets his rocks off associating with collegiate sports. I'm a coach who wants to get back to coaching."[103]

In fact, Moglia wasn't planning to do the unpaid intern thing forever. He hoped to become a college assistant coach and maybe even a head coach. But then in 2010, almost out of nowhere, his football career took another lucky bounce. The pros—in the form of the fledgling United Football League—came calling. The five-team league offered Moglia the head coaching job at its expansion Virginia franchise. Moglia readily accepted and prepared to move back east.

The story got even stranger. The Omaha franchise of the UFL—the league's most successful, with a completely sold-out first season in 2010—fired its head coach. The UFL, which owns its teams, offered the job to Moglia. He would be staying in Nebraska after all.

As of this writing, there continues to be questions about the viability of the UFL, but the new coach and his Omaha Nighthawks are pressing on. In fact, Moglia, who continues

---

102 Ibid.

103 Ibid.

to serve as chairman of the board of TD Ameritrade, has been hinting that he may purchase the Omaha franchise himself and bring more financial stability to the team and the league.

One thing is certain: the Omaha Nighthawks will continue to play before sold-out crowds, especially because their home is now the brand-new ballpark built in downtown Omaha primarily for the annual College World Series: TD Ameritrade Park.

Shaping Up

Her motivation was simple: she didn't like visible panty lines, she didn't like uncomfortable thongs, and she didn't like the feel and fit of pantyhose. Yes, we're talking about women's undergarments. And we're talking about a young woman who took a passion for everyday style and comfort and parlayed it into an incredibly successful clothing line and her own celebrity career. We're talking about Sara Blakely and Spanx.

Today Spanx is a multimillion-dollar clothing business, both online and in stores, and its young creator and founder is riding that incredible wave of fame and fortune. But fame and fortune were nowhere to be found in the company's early days. There was just Sara Blakely's relentless passion, her fearless drive to make it happen no matter how hard the work and how discouraging the results.

Blakely, now 40, was born and raised in Clearwater, Florida. She earned a degree in communications from

Florida State, failed the law school entrance exam, and went to work selling copy machines. She was on a ho-hum path to nowhere. But her passion and energy needed an outlet. She had $5,000 in savings and found something near and dear to her—underwear—to focus on. She didn't like the way her pantyhose fit and looked on her, and she was determined to invent a new way of dressing up underneath.

She did the research every time she had a few spare minutes to get online. She kept her day job for a while and even worked evenings as a stand-up comedian. She read books on patents and trademarks at a Georgia Tech library (she had relocated to the Peach State), zeroing in on the pantyhose industry. She met with lawyers to go over her plans and schemes. Some of them, she reports, thought her idea "was so crazy that they later admitted thinking I had been sent by *Candid Camera.*"[104]

But Sara Blakely wasn't fooling. She wrote the patent herself, got it approved, and successfully trademarked the name "Spanx" online. Her research about brands had told her that a *k* sound was often effective. She came up with "Spanks," which had an obvious cute twist in the context of undergarments. Her research had also told her made-up words for brands do well, so she dropped the *k* and replaced it with the *x*, giving her a name that met both criteria.

So she had a name, but she still didn't have a physical product. She took a week off from her day job and drove

---

104 "Sara's Story," spanx.com, http://www.spanx.com/corp/index.jsp?page=saras Story&clickId=sarasstory_aboutsara_text.

to North Carolina textile mills to pitch her underwear idea directly to hosiery manufacturers. Most just shook their heads and sent her on her way. But one manufacturer didn't ("I have two daughters," he told her) and began working with Blakely to create the prototype for Spanx—a footless, body-shaping, sheer, comfortable undergarment for the women of today and tomorrow. The Spanx slimming technology "provides graduated compression throughout the leg for improved circulation and all-day support."[105] That's the promise and the Spanx prototype delivered.

Blakely came up with bold packaging for her Spanx—bright red with an illustration of three women on the front and the sassy tagline, "Don't worry, we've got your butt covered." So she had the prototype and the packaging. Now she needed an outlet, a place to sell them. She went big, calling a Neiman Marcus buyer, flying to Dallas to meet with her, modeling a Spanx garment herself, and closing the deal. Neiman Marcus said yes and stocked Blakely's creation. She made similar trips to other giant retailers, including Saks, Nordstrom, and Bloomingdale's. At each stop she was both model and pitch person. They all said yes. Her passion had paid off.

But she didn't take a breath; she didn't slow down. She had no budget for advertising, so she hit the road, visiting store after store to pitch Spanx to sales associates and customers. "I became notorious for lifting up my pant leg to every woman walking by," she remembers. "My mom always said that

---

105 "Apparel," spanx.com, http://www.spanx.com/category/index.jsp?categoryId =2992556&ab=Apparel_Nav.

as long as I lifted my pants up and not down to show my product then I had her blessing."[106]

Blakely and her friends and family members relentlessly pitched Spanx to news outlets, hoping to get some free PR. And did they ever. Spanx and Blakely were featured on *The Oprah Winfrey Show*, *The Today Show*, *The View*, *The Tyra Banks Show*, and countless local TV programs. Her list of print coverage is just as impressive: *Forbes*, *Fortune*, *People*, *Entrepreneur*, *InStyle*, *The New York Times*, *USA Today*, *Glamour*, *Vogue*, and many more. Then reality television came calling. Blakely appeared on *The Rebel Billionaire: Branson's Quest for the Best*, even having tea in a hot air balloon with Richard Branson. The three-month *Rebel Billionaire* gig took her to China, London, and South Africa, where she spent an afternoon with Mr. and Mrs. Nelson Mandela.

Again, Blakely showed her relentlessness and passion. Not only did she use her time with Branson to tell him all about her company and herself, she also shared her dream of helping the women of Africa as they struggle against the cultural forces that keep them down. Branson was impressed. At the end of the show, Branson handed Blakely a check for $750,000—his pay from Fox for the series—so she could pursue her dream. Branson was there in Atlanta in 2006 when Blakely launched the Sara Blakely Foundation, dedicated to helping women globally through education and entrepreneurship.

Meanwhile, her company continues to grow and expand

---

106 "Sara's Story," spanx.com, http://www.spanx.com/corp/index.jsp?page=saras Story&clickId=sarasstory_aboutsara_text.

the product line, adding Assets (created exclusively for Target), Spanx Power Panties, and Spanx High-Falutin' Foot- less Pantyhose. And there'll be plenty more where those came from—all because a smart, creative, passionate woman from Florida didn't like the look and feel of her underwear.

Mirror Image

Our third and final example of a person in the fearless and crazy pursuit of a personal passion is not a famous celebrity, politician, sports star, or CEO. It's not someone from the history books or the *Forbes* list of the richest. Yet it's someone you are quite familiar with. Look in the mirror. It's *you*.

Like Joe Moglia and Sara Blakely, you have personal passions you'd love to pursue. You have dreams, you have ambitions, and you have things you'd like to do, things you'd like to try.

In his book *Turn Your Passion into Profit*, business writer Walt F. J. Goodridge, himself a fearless and crazy "nomadpreneur" who travels the world for work and play, uses a clever acronym, LIFE PASSION, to show the qualities of passion, be it personal, professional, or a mix of both.

L **LOVE:** Your passion is something you love to do.

I **INTEREST:** Your passion is something that interests you.

F **FULFILLING:** Your passion gives you a sense of fulfillment.

E **EMPOWERING:** Your passion usually empowers and energizes you.

P **PERSONAL:** Your passion has personal significance to you and you alone.

A **ABILITIES:** Your passion capitalizes on your assets, attributes, and abilities.

S **SERVICE:** Your passion will usually provide a service or fulfill a need.

S **SPIRITUAL:** Your passion and its pursuit represent an area of spiritual growth.

I **INSPIRING:** Your passion is inspiring to you and therefore will inspire others too.

O **OBVIOUS:** Your passion, once found, is usually something obvious to you.

N **NATURAL:** Your passion is often unstudied and comes naturally to you.[107]

That all makes sense, but maybe life keeps getting in the way of your passion. Sure, some people can just drop everything and run off to join the circus, but you have obligations and responsibilities. Maybe you have a home and family. Maybe you have an office or a warehouse filled with hardworking employees dependent on you. Or maybe it's just that you've got bills to pay—every month, every day. Those aren't going away, and you should never shirk your moral obligations.

So the passion, the dream, is set aside, pushed into the corners of your mind. You most likely won't ever open that

---

107 Walt F. J. Goodridge, *Turn Your Passion into Profit* (New York: Passion Profit, 2010), 101.

restaurant. You most likely won't ever climb Mt. Everest. You most likely won't ever join the Peace Corps.

But don't throw your passion away, ever. You can chip away at it; you can work on it on the side. Maybe your dream was to be a Hollywood screenwriter, but life got in the way. Well, get in there and do some of it anyway. Buy a screen-writing how-to book. Take a screenwriting course at your local community college. Join a writers group. Start writing. Keep writing. Maybe just a half hour or an hour a day, late at night or early in the morning. Enter your script in one of the many screenwriting contests. Should you rehearse your Oscar acceptance speech? No. And you most likely won't sell a script. But you will be answering the siren's call of your personal passion.

Maybe you've always wanted to cook, to be a chef. You wanted to open your own little bistro in an upscale part of town and have some amazing and unusual specials of the day to write on your chalkboard at the front door. But then life got in the way—spouse, kids, bills, bills, and more bills. You don't have to shoo the dream away. You can dabble in it, as time and circumstances permit. Take a culinary course at a local college. Host a series of dinners at your home for special friends and family members. Join a club of like-minded chefs. Maybe create a blog for recipe sharing or local restaurant news. Will you have your own show on Food Network? Nope. But you will be answering the siren's call of your personal passion.

You will be experiencing the rush that comes from writing, cooking, setting up shop, forming a partnership—any creative endeavor. And because you are at least engaging with your passion, your entire frame of mind and your confidence will improve. You'll feel better about yourself. Your friends and family members will notice the difference. You'll perform your obligations and responsibilities better and will enjoy them more. Following your personal passion, even if only part way—even if it's only a toe in the water—is good for the soul.

Someone might say, "You get up at five A.M. and write stuff every day? What are you, crazy?"

Or they might say, "You're going to a cooking class on Monday nights when you could be watching football? What are you, crazy?"

Writing, cooking—whatever that passion is—you'll answer, "Yeah, a little." And then you'll smile.

■ ■ ■

➡ MY TAKE

Let's talk about courage—the courage to pursue a personal passion, the courage to accept and perform your personal responsibilities, and the courage to be fearless and crazy. Aristotle called courage the first of human qualities "because it is the quality which guarantees the others." What follows may sound a little preachy at times, but it's important. It's very near and dear to my heart. In fact, if I had to say in one word what this book is about, that word would be *courage*.

In animals, fear is the key to what scientists call the fight-or-flight response, which is necessary for survival. In human beings, too, fear is a natural response to a perceived or real threat. Being conscious of fears, and subsequently of any threats, is a good thing. The advantage of being fearless, though, is that you don't exactly ignore your fears but instead act to bring them under control and keep them in check. 187 Your ability to do this—to control your fears—is one of the things that makes you human. It is part of living consciously; you make decisions based on rational thought rather than allowing your instincts to govern how you act. And in business, for obvious reasons, this is crucial.

By living consciously and investing in every decision you make—by planning ahead—you put yourself in a position to achieve. You have a choice: either exercise your human courage and consciousness or admit that your fears are too much for you and embrace a life on the sidelines. But make this choice deliberately and with full awareness of its consequences.

Courage is the very essence of life-wealth. It is necessary at every step—vision, planning, execution, marketing, networking, and dealing with the unknowns. If you decide to be courageous and embark on a life-wealth path of personal development, a path that will see you on your way to living consciously and achieving your goals, you should also keep in mind, for the long run, that you may endure dysfunctional relationships, you may be broke at one time or another, and you may even fail completely. It's impossible to predict what will happen, even if you work hard and plan hard. But don't be put off. Even the most devastating failures are all just obstacles along the path of a life lived courageously. You'll always have your private victory as a conscious person, with an abundance of joy, happiness, and fulfillment in your life.

Courageous people are still afraid, but they work to prevent their fears from paralyzing them. Giving in to your fears causes the long-term, unintended effect of strengthening them; similarly, when you avoid your fears and feel relieved that you don't have to deal with them for now, you accept a psychological reward that reinforces the avoidance behavior. You are all the more likely to avoid the fears in the future. You condition yourself to become timid and to ignore challenges that might lead to success. Unless you nip this behavior in the bud, you block yourself from ever achieving your goals.

Avoidance behavior causes stagnation in the long run, and as you get older, it becomes harder and harder even to imagine yourself standing up to your fears, let alone actually doing so. You cocoon yourself in your life, whether it's in an unhappy marriage, an unsatisfying job, or a too-low income bracket. You're smothered and not living the life you dreamed of. So you accept it, and you give up.

But don't do it. There's a voice in the back of your head telling you every day that you can be successful, and it's time that you heeded it. It's like the unmuffled voice you heard when you were a child or a teen and had your whole life in front of you—seemingly without limits, wide open. Like most people as they grow older, you settled into avoiding your fears and accepting a pattern for your life that doesn't require any effort. You switched off or drowned out the little voice. And you still try not to hear it as it tells you that it's still possible to make a fortune or rebuild a relationship, that it's not too late to learn new skills or start your own business.

Perhaps you drown out that voice by watching television, working long hours, or drinking alcohol or caffeine. Some drown it out by overeating or undereating. Whatever your drug of choice happens to be, it's important to identify it and, if you're serious about achieving any of your goals, put a stop to it right away. Whenever you muffle that little voice telling you to do better, you're lowering your level of consciousness. You're moving closer to becoming an instinctive animal and further away from becoming a conscious human being. You react to life instead of proactively going after your goals. You fall into a state of learned helplessness.

Putting an end to the vicious cycle means summoning your courage and confronting that inner voice. Sit down with a pen and a piece of paper. You're going to make a list. Use your computer if you wish, but I prefer doing it the old-fashioned way—ink on paper. Writing something out can more easily bring a spiritual release of your feelings. Think about what the little voice in your head is saying now and what it has been saying for years. Write down everything about your aspirations and your dreams. Be general or specific, write a long list or a short one—it doesn't matter. Just so you write something down. You are at the first stage of life-wealth: vision.

As you're looking over your list and mulling your possibilities, think of these words from Ralph Waldo Emerson: "Whatever you do, you need courage. Whatever course you decide upon, there is always someone to tell you that you are wrong. There are always difficulties arising that tempt you to believe your critics are right. To map out a course of action and follow it to an end requires some of the same courage that a soldier needs. Peace has its victories, but it takes brave men and women to win them."[108]

---

108 "Emerson: Quotes," transcendentalists.com, http://www.transcendentalists.com/emerson_quotes.htm.

And consider this from writer Steve Pavlina: "Fear is not your enemy. It is a compass pointing you to the areas where you need to grow. So when you encounter a new fear within yourself, celebrate it as an opportunity for growth, just as you would celebrate reaching a new personal best with strength training."[109] As author Erica Jong writes, "Everyone has a talent. What is rare is the courage to follow the talent to the dark place where it leads."[110]

After you realize exactly what your fearless dream is, after you accept and embrace that wild and crazy dream, it's time for the planning phase, the second step on the life-wealth path. Planning is fundamental because it gives you a relatively stress-free context for working out many of the problems you are likely to encounter as you execute your idea. As you plan, you are conscious of those problems, you are analyzing them, and you are prepping yourself for them. In fact, you are incrementally developing the courage you will need later.

You develop courage gradually, just as if it were a muscle in your body. You'll be able to take on increasingly bigger challenges because your courage will become conditioned like any other muscle you decide to train consistently and conscientiously over time. If you don't work your muscles regularly, you become weak both physically and mentally. If you don't regularly exercise your courage, you strengthen your fear by default, and your courage decays.

---

109 Steve Pavlina, "The Courage to Live Consciously," StevePavlina.com, http://www.stevepavlina.com/articles/courage-to-live-consciously.htm.

110 Erica Jong, "The Artist as Housewife," in *The First Ms. Reader*, ed. Francine Klagsbrun (New York: Warner Paperback Library, 1973), 113.

But remember, being courageous, planning, and then living your fearless and crazy dream doesn't give you the right to be foolhardy, irresponsible, or harmful. Sometimes the best-laid fearless and crazy plans turn out to be disasters—flat-out dangerous for you or others. If that happens or you even see it coming, then put on the brakes. Being fearless and crazy is not a license to do harm. Put another way, regardless of who you are and where you are in your own life, you have a responsibility to take care of, at the very least, your own basic needs. You need a place to live, food to eat, clothes to wear, and the means to maintain your health. Most of us carry even greater responsibilities in that we have families and loved ones who rely on us.

Now you have created a life-wealth road map for every waking minute of your life from now on. You have set goals for yourself and established a plan of action so that you know how you are going to pursue your fearless and crazy vision. Next, you take that first step, and the fun begins.

As Dale Carnegie put it, "Inaction breeds doubt and fear. Action breeds confidence and courage. If you want to conquer fear, do not sit home and think about it. Go out and get busy."[111]

Well, you heard the man. Get busy!

---

111 Dale Carnegie Quotes, quotes-clothing.com, http://www.quotes-clothing.com/inaction-doubt-fear-action-confidence-courage-get-busy-dale-carnegie/.

10

YOUR TURN, YOUR STEPS, YOUR FUTURE

I've been rich and I've been poor. Rich is better.

SOPHIE TUCKER

I n Chapter 1 you get an overview of my life-wealth plan. In the introduction and the postscript you learn a little about how I have embraced that plan and used it in my professional and personal career. And of course, in all those chapters in between, you read about so many others—most of them business success stories, some of them historical figures or sports legends. That's all well and good, you say, but how do I get started? How do I embrace life-wealth? Get a pencil or a pen, and read on.

To review, the components of my life-wealth plan are:

- ➠ Vision
- ➠ Planning
- ➠ Execution
- ➠ Marketing
- ➠ Networking
- ➠ Dealing with the unknown

It's time for you to put on paper some of the ideas that have surely been banging around in your head as you have read these pages. The following are my learning tools for the life-wealth components. They will help you put your ideas in writing.

The Vision Builder

Your short-term, mid-term, and long-term goals must be in the front of your mind every day. You need to see them, be reminded of them, and think about them. They are part of you and what you will be. Have them on your smart phone, your iPad, your screensaver, your mirror, your bulletin board, and your refrigerator. And take them a step further. Ask yourself the following questions, and write down your answers somewhere you can keep track of them:

- ➠ Where do you *want to be* in (a) 1 year, (b) 5 years, and (c) 10 years?
- ➠ Where do you want to be living?
- ➠ What do you want to be doing?
- ➠ Who do you want to be with?
- ➠ How much money do you want to have in savings?

➡ How do you want to be making money?

➡ How much debt do you want to have?

➡ Where are you *now*—personally, professionally, and financially?

➡ Where do you live?

➡ What do you do?

➡ Who are you with?

➡ How much money do you have in savings?

➡ How are you making money?

➡ How much debt do you have?

➡ Are you paying cash or charging large purchases, such as cars, furniture, and vacations?

Continue by listing your goals in the format below and answering the probing questions that follow.

Short-term goals: 1 year or less (List these goals no matter how small and minor they may seem.)

1. _____

2. _____

3. _____

Mid-term goals: between 1 year and 10 years

1. _____

2. _____

3. _____

Long-term goals: 10 years or more

1. _____

2. _____

3. _____

➥ Compare your present state to your vision of the future. What in particular do you need to change about your current situation to progress toward achieving your vision of the future?

➥ Keeping in mind what you learned previously about having passion and purpose associated with your vision, ask yourself the following questions:

  • What vision "owns" your mind when you go to sleep?
  • What vision "owns" your mind when you wake up in the middle of the night?
  • What vision are you thinking about while you're at work?
  • What is the one thing you tell all your friends about?
  • What is the one thing you spend all your time researching on the Internet?

Armed with these lists, you should be able to write a short paragraph about your vision for the future, why it is important to you, and why you are motivated to pursue it. This paragraph can basically serve as your mission statement or a statement of your intentions. It's what you are hoping to achieve and why.

Power Planning

Timeliness is crucial when it comes to effective planning. When you have a goal you hope to achieve, you need to give yourself a clear plan of action and a time frame for that action. Consider the following questions:

A. What is the goal?

_____

B. What is the plan to achieve the goal? (Remember, fearless and crazy is okay; the first step can be bold.)

Step 1: _____

Step 2: _____

Step 3: _____

C. What is the time frame for achieving the goal?

_____

For each of the three steps of the plan, answer the following questions:

1. What is the step in the plan?

   _____

2. What is the time frame for executing that step?

   _____

3. What needs to happen for you to be able to start execution?

   _____

4. What strategies can you employ to stay motivated to execute your plan?

   _____

5. How will you monitor progress toward the achievement of your goals?

   _____

With this information in hand, you should have a clear idea about how to execute your plans. You should also have at least a couple of strategies in mind to help you stay motivated and focused. Although you may pick up some momentum after taking the first step, remember it is just as important to follow through as it is to get started. It's all very well to be fearless and crazy, but you have to sustain the fearlessness and the craziness throughout the execution of your plan if you are going to succeed.

Learning Tool for Execution

As that trite old saying goes, a journey of a thousand miles begins with the first step. Here's a significant first step you can take to begin the execution of your plan. It's one we first touched on in Chapter 4. It's about debt and credit, and to many people it's not only fearless, it's downright crazy.

I got my start using credit cards, but I later did a 180 and worked to free myself from indebtedness. To make my short-term, mid-term, and long-term goals reality, I cut up my credit cards, conserved my capital, and paid cash whenever and wherever I could. That included paying for the big stuff like a house, cars, and college educations. Now I have the ability and freedom to go after my dreams not feeling liable to anybody, not having payments and due dates hanging over me. When you don't have debt, you're not in bondage. So get crazily and fearlessly out of debt so you can be the person God meant for you to be. Don't owe—you owe it to yourself not to.

To put it bluntly, do not use credit cards.

Yes, I know it sounds impossible, but hear me out.

Certainly, there are many ways to increase revenue in business—most basically, sell more products or services. But how can you reduce and control the amount of debt you have, either professionally or personally?

Answer: stop using your credit cards.

Do I mean scale back the use of your credit cards?

Answer: no, stop using them *completely*. Now.

How do you do that?

Answer: cut those cards into very small pieces, and distribute those pieces in several different trash cans.

If you're truly committed to reducing your debt until it has been totally wiped out, if you're truly committed to building real wealth for today and tomorrow, and if you're truly committed to changing your life forever, cut those credit cards into pieces right now.

However, you may consider keeping one *charge* card such as an American Express card. A charge card does not allow you to extend your indebtedness to the card company. It's unlike a typical credit card in that the full balance is due when you get the bill. There's no minimum payment option and no partial-pay option. A charge card is appropriate for travel, especially business travel. It can be a valuable tool when you're on the road, especially in a foreign country.

In addition, you might want to spare one credit card from the wrath of your scissors. But it can be only one, and it must have substantial unused credit available. This card is for emergencies—genuine, real, gut-wrenching emergencies. Being out of chardonnay is not an emergency. Craving your favorite fast food is not an emergency. Wanting to bet $6 on an exacta box at the track is not an emergency. In fact, this emergencies-only credit card should not be carried on your person or—heaven forbid—in your car's glove box. Keep it tucked somewhere safely at home so that when you do consider using it, you have to make an effort to retrieve it. That effort may allow you time to rethink the severity of the emergency at hand. But serious emergencies do happen, and they are not fun. This special card can be important.

If you can do this—cut up those cards except for one tucked away for emergencies—you'll be taking a giant step forward toward financial freedom and peace of mind. Carrying cash is the companion to that giant step. If you have only cash on you, you will have second thoughts every time you take out money to pay for something. You'll hesitate for just a quick, prudent moment because you can only spend what is in your wallet or purse. If your purchase is purely an impulse item, such as Chinese takeout or that on-sale sweater, you may decide it's not worth spending the money, even if it's only a few bucks. When you lay out the cash for something, you immediately see and feel that wad of bills shrink. You immediately and unequivocally know that you have just reduced your wealth. Sound cheap? Yup, and that's the idea. It's part of thinking wealthy. It's part of my life-wealth campaign.

You may not feel comfortable carrying cash, of course. There are the obvious safety concerns. Perhaps a *debit* card is the card for you. The credit card processing companies treat them almost the same as credit cards. One difference is that these companies charge a substantially lower fee to the merchants for debit purchases than for credit card purchases. Why? Because the money is drawn immediately from your account at the time of purchase. No credit card company is giving you a "float" or lending you money.

When you use plastic—credit or debit—you're playing in a financial institution's game by a financial institution's rules.

I realize the recent spate of consumer protection regulations and restrictions has cleared up a lot of confusion, done away with a lot of legalese, and greatly aided customers and merchants alike. I certainly applaud all of that. But the cynic in me knows that the card companies and their institutional masters will soon find ways around those protections and will come up with some new wrinkles to increase their piece of your pie.

Once you get off the credit card merry-go-round and start paying cash for things, you'll notice several pleasant lifestyle changes in a very short period of time. You will be making fewer purchases in general and a lot fewer impulse purchases in particular. Your existing credit card statements will have fewer transaction lines and a smaller bottom line with each new payment you make. If you had debt on a card, you're paying it down; you're lifting the financial burden. And of course, you'll find more of what I call "unspent discretionary income" accumulating in your checking account, your savings account, and even your wallet or purse. It's obvious but true nonetheless: you're spending less and saving more. In terms of our life-wealth discussion, a cash strategy will allow you to better execute the other achievables of your plan, give you more resources for marketing and networking, and better prepare you to deal with the unknowns.

You'll look back and wonder why you ever got on that credit card merry-go-round in the first place. A cash-only philosophy may seem like something from decades ago— certainly not a typical 21st-century wealth strategy. But that's the fearless and crazy beauty of it; it's against type. I should know; I made the switch.

Learning Tool for Marketing and Networking 203

I've combined these two life-wealth components in one basic tool because they go hand in hand. When you're marketing, you're networking—maybe with one acquaintance, maybe with one million consumers. Similarly, when you're networking, you're marketing—yourself (Product You), your company, and your idea. Marketing and networking are different sides of the same coin.

In Chapter 8 you learned (or relearned) about SWOT analysis as a simple, effective tool for analyzing yourself as you map out your marketing path. You read various SWOT examples, including mine. Now it's time to do a SWOT analysis of yourself, a particular business of yours, or a specific opportunity you are mulling:

What are the strengths?

- _____

- _____

- _____

- _____

- _____

What are the weaknesses?

- _____

- _____

- _____

What are the opportunities?

- _____

- _____

- _____

What are the threats?

- _____

- _____

- _____

On the basis of your answers, decide whether this is an opportunity or situation worth pursuing, or if you are conducting a personal SWOT analysis, decide whether you are the right person to take on the opportunity or situation in question.

Now answer the following questions to develop your marketing and networking plan even further and to prepare yourself for specific marketing and networking opportunities.

1. **What are the goals of your marketing and networking activity or activities?**

    Goal 1: _____

    Goal 2: _____

    Goal 3: _____

2. **How do you get there?**

    What do you need to do to achieve goal 1?

    _____

    What do you need to do to achieve goal 2?

    _____

    What do you need to do to achieve goal 3?

    _____

3. **Who is your audience?**

    _____

4. What's the key message you need to get across to your audience?

_____

5. What can you do to engage the people you're meeting with or presenting to? What few key words or important concepts should you make sure to include in the conversation or presentation?

_____

6. What can you do to build a relationship, not simply make a sale in the context of your meeting?

_____

7. What do you want out of the situation? What is the question you need to ask to get what you want?

_____

8. What is your plan to follow up on the meeting within 24 to 48 hours?

_____

9. What can you do to help yourself relax before, during, and after the meeting? Think of a couple of strategies that will help you stay focused and calm during the exchange.

_____

Learning Tool for Dealing with the Unknown   207

The traps, the surprises, the setbacks, the acts of God and nature—we know they're out there, ready to trip us up and send us crashing down. The trouble is we never know when, where, or even if. So you've got to be ready. You've got to have backup plans. This tool will get you not only thinking of those backups but mapping them out as well.

First, identify the key variables that might threaten your vision and goals or cause your initial plans to fail.

Variable 1: _____

Variable 2: _____

Variable 3: _____

Take note of your financial resources. What backup resources do you have? Consider:

1. Backup funds:

_____

2. Backup credit:

_____

3. Other backup resources:

_____

After compiling this information, identify alternative
plans for achieving your goals:

Alternative plan for goal 1:

_____

Alternative plan for goal 2:

_____

Alternative plan for goal 3:

_____

Identify at least one backup plan for each of your goals, and take note if you can of several possible alternative strategies to achieve your end goal. Although you may want to play it safe with your backup plans, try to incorporate fearless and crazy principles here as well. Your backup plans don't have to be quite as daring as your original plans, but they should be innovative and solid.

The Crazy and Fearless Persona Builder

This final tool doesn't correspond directly to the components of my life-wealth plan, but it is crucial to everything in these pages. It's about you becoming more like the fearless and crazy people you met here, including yours truly.

To develop a fitting persona for your fearless and crazy ventures, try the following:

List your top three personality traits (i.e., describe what people notice first about you):

1. _____

2. _____

3. _____

List the top three traits you want to develop to be more effective in business (e.g., confidence, resolve, focus):

1. _____

2. _____

3. _____

To develop the traits in the second list, compare the two lists, and think about which of your natural traits might need to change for you to take on that fearless and crazy persona that will make you more effective in business. For example, if you are normally a shy person or you get stage fright when you are making presentations, think about developing a persona that exudes confidence and allows you to be over the top in situations that would normally make you feel embarrassed or uncomfortable. Think about whether dressing a certain way or having certain accessories is going to help you develop the personality traits that will make you more effective.

It's this kind of analysis—these sorts of lists—that will get you started on the crazy and fearless path. Visit www.crazy-andfearless.com for even more about that path.

Take these first steps; go where so many of us have already gone and continue to travel. You'll soon discover how exciting and energizing it can be. You'll soon develop your own unique version of a life-wealth plan. You'll soon experience success.

11

WELL SAID

Wise men make proverbs, but fools repeat them.

—SAMUEL PALMER

If you've come with me this far through these fearless and crazy pages, I've got a small reward for you: words, powerful words, strung into sentences that have meaning and shed light. You've certainly noticed along the way that I am a fan of the well-said remark or the inspirational saying. What follows are a few more of my favorites about being fearless and crazy, about taking risks, and about conquering fears. Find one that you especially like, and put it in your wallet or purse, post it on your bulletin board, or sticky-note it to your computer monitor. Read it frequently or from time to time. If it's a good one for you, it will give a boost when you need it. It will keep you going when you want to quit. It will keep your eyes on the prize.

Why not go out on a limb? Isn't that where the fruit is?

—FRANK SCULLY

You'll always miss 100 percent of the shots you don't take.

—WAYNE GRETZKY

Only those who dare to fail greatly can ever achieve greatly.

—ROBERT F. KENNEDY

It is not because things are difficult that we do not dare; it is because we do not dare that they are difficult.

—SENECA

Dare to be naive.

—R. BUCKMINSTER FULLER

One does not discover new lands without consenting to lose sight of the shore for a very long time.

—ANDRÉ GIDE

Living at risk is jumping off the cliff and building your wings
on the way down.

—RAY BRADBURY

Courage is being scared to death but saddling up anyway.

—JOHN WAYNE

Shoot for the moon. Even if you miss, you'll land among the stars.

—LES BROWN

Excellence is not a skill. It is an attitude.

RALPH MARSTON

I am always doing that which I cannot do, in order that I may
learn how to do it.

—PABLO PICASSO

Success comes in cans, not can'ts.

—UNKNOWN

Look not mournfully into the past. It comes not back again.
Wisely improve the present. It is thine. Go forth to meet the
shadowy future, without fear.

—HENRY WADSWORTH LONGFELLOW

Opportunity is missed by most people because it is dressed in overalls and looks like work.

—THOMAS EDISON

Nobody ever drowned in his own sweat.

—ANN LANDERS

You have to risk going too far to discover just how far you can really go.

—T. S. ELIOT

People who don't take risks generally make about two big mistakes a year. People who do take risks generally make about two big mistakes a year.

—PETER F. DRUCKER

Progress always involves risks. You can't steal second base and keep your foot on first.

—FREDERICK B. WILCOX

Life is being on the wire; everything else is just waiting.

—KARL WALLENDA

Do one thing every day that scares you.

—ELEANOR ROOSEVELT

POSTSCRIPT

In this book's introduction, I told you about my fearless and crazy decision to move to the Detroit area and set up my film studio, make great movies, and become a rich and famous producer. The decision was especially clever and smart because the state of Michigan offered refundable tax credits of up to 42 percent to filmmakers. In effect, the state would be paying me to do what I wanted to do anyway—make movies.

Well, not so fast, Arthur Wylie. With most states under so much budget pressure, I guess it should have come as no surprise that Michigan would rethink its generous enticement for filmmakers. And that's just what Governor Rick Snyder did. In spring 2011, he proposed capping the incentives at $25 million starting in 2012. This may sound like a lot of money, but scores of Michigan film projects each year apply for more than $100 million in credits. In fact, in 2009, the total was about $133 million; in 2010, it was about $198 million. So a $25 million cap would mean a very small pie for filmmakers to cut up.

Not only was the governor's incentive cap gaining traction, the Michigan legislature was putting up little or no resistance, with some lawmakers even wanting to drop the incentives altogether. The handwriting was clearly on the wall—written in ink. The tax credits were important elements in our strategy and those of other Michigan filmmakers, potentially affecting everything from a project pro forma to a company business plan. So what should we do about the new playing field in Michigan?

Unfortunately and regrettably, we and just about every other filmmaker in Michigan had to find a new playing field. For us, that field was Louisiana. The tax credit in Louisiana is about 30 percent—low compared to Michigan's 42 percent. But there is no overall cap in Louisiana, and there will not be one. The state appreciates the power and potential of the movie industry and is doing everything it can to foster that industry's growth. Louisiana sees itself as "Hollywood East"—if not now, soon. So we packed up and headed to Cajun Country. And then the story got very interesting.

On a flight from the Dominican Republic one long travel day in the spring of 2011, I was dismayed when in the last few minutes before takeoff I was bumped from first class to coach. Oh well. It happens. I put myself in a zombie frame of mind, slipped on my sunglasses, fastened my seat belt, and decided to just get through it. Mindless and numb until touchdown. But after a few polite pleasantries with my seatmate, an unexpected thing happened. We struck up a conversation. A good one. So good, in fact, it may end up being the most important in-flight chat of my life.

He introduced himself as Scott Steele, and I learned that

he's the executive director of an organization called Cherokee Gives Back. It's the philanthropic arm of Cherokee Invest- ment Partners, a private equity investment firm focused on brownfield redevelopment and sustainable real estate investments. *Brownfield* means just what the word implies: abandoned or underused industrial or commercial sites available for reuse. That redevelopment or reuse may be complicated by the presence or potential presence of a hazardous substance, pollutant, or contaminant at the site. Cherokee takes what has been written off and writes it a brand-new story.

In fact, Cherokee is the leading private equity firm dedicating its capital and expertise to brownfield redevelopment. Cherokee has invested in more than 525 properties worldwide. The firm has nearly $2 billion under management and is currently investing its fourth fund. Not only does Cherokee reclaim, restore, and reuse those forgotten tracts of land and crumbling facilities, it does so always aware of environmental and sustainability issues. Cherokee is very green and very proud of it. In 2000, it created Cherokee Gives Back. The organization has helped nonprofit and community-based initiatives in the United States, Ethiopia, Rwanda, Romania, Russia, China, and India.

Steele told me all this and more as the jet's engines hummed and the flight attendants made their way up and down the aisle. And he told me where Cherokee has been focusing so much of its efforts in the past few years: New Orleans. That's right, Louisiana, my new filmmaking home. It makes sense for Cherokee; think of the brownfield opportunities and needs in and around the Crescent City in the wake of the 2005 Katrina nightmare.

I didn't just listen to Scott Steele on that flight; I talked a bit too. I told him about myself, my investment career, and my filmmaking goals. As I talked and listened, I was thinking about how my Global Renaissance Entertainment enterprise and his enterprise—both the parent company and its Gives Back branch—might work together. I focused on what they might need that I could provide. As discussed in Chapter 6, I tried to see challenges and opportunities from their vantage point. I looked for ways I could help them meet their goals. It's the most powerful and effective networking there is. It's the opposite of selfish and self-centered. You find opportunities to help the other guys, and in doing so, you end up helping yourself.

Global Renaissance Entertainment Group and Cherokee are now working together in Louisiana to not only make movies but expand their brownfield work. I have developed a strong business relationship and friendship with Cherokee CEO Tom Darden. They will help me jump-start my own charitable foundation. With their real estate expertise, they will assist me as I pursue my dream of creating a film school in the state. With my wealth management expertise, I will help them invest and grow their assets. A true partnership has been born.

Much of the work we do will be green—eco-friendly, conservation-aware, sustainable, and responsible. In fact, since 2007, Steele's Cherokee Gives Back has been partnering with Brad Pitt, GRAFT, and William McDonough + Partners as part of the Make It Right project to build 150 green, storm-resistant, affordable homes in New Orleans's Lower 9th Ward, the neighborhood most damaged by Hurricane

Katrina. You know who Brad Pitt is, of course. GRAFT is a Los Angeles–based architecture and design firm that goes far beyond the mere building of structures, "grafting" cross-cultural influences and interdisciplinary components onto everything they do. And Bill McDonough is one of the foremost green architects and community designers in the world. His book *Cradle to Cradle* is the definitive work on green architecture and planning.

So for yours truly, it's almost showtime. We've got a couple of feature films in development; we're working with the folks who produced the successful *Final Destination* movie series. We're launching Omar Tyree's *Flyy Girl* for television. I'm even doing some screenwriting myself.

Yes, Detroit, Michigan, was a fearless and crazy decision, and I ended up swinging and missing, just like we discuss in Chapter 8. But now I'm into something huge, something important, the opportunity of my young lifetime. If you'd like to monitor what I'm up to, visit www.arthurwylie.com. And to comment about these pages and this book, visit www.crazyandfearless.com.

Now, I know you're thinking: *Yeah, Arthur, you were just lucky. When I sit down next to someone on a plane, it's either a gray-haired lady with pictures of her grandkids or a salesman from Peoria who wants to fight me for the armrest.*

Well, sure, there was some luck involved. I certainly didn't want to get bumped from first class. But remember, I know how to network effectively. I put myself in the other person's shoes; I see the situation from the other person's perspective. Then I look for ways I can help that person achieve his goals, meet his targets, or overcome his obstacles. I problem-solve

for him, offering myself as his solution. I did it with Scott
Steele that day. And you know what? He did it with me. We
found the synergy, and now we're running with it.

So is it all just too crazy? Maybe.

Is it fearless? You bet.

ACKNOWLEDGMENTS

I want to dedicate this book to my son, William Arthur Wylie III (Trey). May he be crazy, fearless, and methodical, while never settling for less than his best. Thank you, The Most High, for your many blessings, for my many experiences, for my wonderful family and friends—despite my many short-comings. Grace, mercy, and forgiveness are amazing. Never be too quick to judge. Patience, passion, and perseverance will do wonders in your life. To all my supporters, colleagues, and fellow entrepreneurs, hopefully this book serves you well and catapults you to the next level. Your involvement in my life has been invaluable.

I also want to thank Brian Nicol for his valuable contribution. Your skills are amazing. A special thank you to the BenBella Books team and its CEO, Glenn Yeffeth. Glenn, you made a great decision signing me up as a first-time author, and I look forward to doing book two!

My inspiration to write this book comes from the late Steve Jobs, Apple founder and technology genius, as well as from many key executives around the world. Critical business partners, family, and friends include Mr. *New York Times*

Best Seller himself, Omar Tyree, Cherokee Funds, Dale God-boldo, Attorney Jeff Miles, Eleanor Earl, all my brokerage and insurance house friends, Richard and Peggy Griffin, UNC-Charlotte, CPCC, and the entire Kennedy family clan (you guys are my heroes!).

I also want to thank my manager, Raoul Davis. He's been with me from day one of this journey. He and his leadership team at Ascendant Strategy are second to none.

Finally, I want to thank all the crazy and fearless entrepreneurs who came before me, those who are brave enough to make the difficult decisions every day. When everyone else says no, you have the courage to say yes!

This book is an evolving, growing testament to day-to-day entrepreneurship, to strategic management, and to finding your way past the challenges and through the roadblocks. Have fun with the book; read it several times; buy one for a friend. It will be an important resource and a dynamic conversation piece for you throughout your crazy and fearless career.

ABOUT THE AUTHORS

"Do the unexpected" is the guiding business philosophy of **Arthur Wylie**, investment mogul, Hollywood executive, serial entrepreneur, and author. This daring mindset prompted him to start his own financial firm out of his college dorm room and to later grow it to oversee hundreds of millions in assets and participate in more than $750 million worth of business deals. This boldness also led him to venture into disparate industries, including the notoriously tough entertainment world, where he has also realized extraordinary success.

Wylie operates outside the box—from scraping up $500 to start his investing company to seamlessly securing a $50 million film-distribution deal. He has become one of the most talked-about entrepreneur brands and youngest success stories in the film industry today. Defying borders and boundaries, Wylie effortlessly manages a diverse business empire that encompasses entertainment/media, financial, and entrepreneurial coaching enterprises.

He has been featured in and on leading national media outlets *The Wall Street* Journal's Market Watch, FOX News,

ABC News, *Forbes* Online, and *Black Enterprise*, among many others.

Among his current endeavors, Wylie is an executive at Global Entertainment Holdings Film Fund, a publicly traded film production firm currently building a $100 million film fund. His duties there range from capital raising, film production oversight, distribution, to marketing, and working with some of Hollywood's top producers who have more than $9 billion in box-office sales.

Wylie holds a bachelor's degree in financial management from the University of North Carolina at Charlotte and has been a licensed securities principal for some of the top investment companies in the world.

Brian Nicol's writing, editing and publishing career spans more than 30 years, most of them in Hawaii, Oregon and Nebraska. He was editor of *Honolulu*, the city and regional magazine of Hawaii, from 1982 until 1990. For a little more than two years, he was editorial director of Aster Publishing Corp. in Eugene, Oregon. From 1992 until 2007, he was CEO of Home & Away Publishing, a AAA-owned media company that produces travel magazines with combined circulation of more than 5.5 million. Nicol is originally from Minnesota and currently resides in Omaha.